Introduction to the

Family

Proceedings

Court

A basic outline of the law and practice of the family proceedings court in England and Wales, produced under the auspices of the Justices' Clerks' Society for use by family panel magistrates and other people interested in the arrangements to provide local justice for children and families

Introduction to the
Family Proceedings Court

Published 1997 by
WATERSIDE PRESS
Domum Road
Winchester SO23 9NN
Telephone or Fax 01962 855567
INTERNET:106025.1020@compuserve.com

ISBN Paperback 1 872 870 46 5

Cataloguing-in-Publication Data A catalogue record for this book can be obtained from the British Library

Cover design John Good Holbrook Ltd, Coventry. Main photograph by kind permission of the Inner London and City Family Proceedings Court. Photograph of Sir Stephen Brown courtesy of the Lord Chancellor's Department.

Printing and binding Antony Rowe Ltd, Chippenham.

Acknowledgments The authors and publishers wish to acknowledge: the provision of materials by the Warwickshire Magistrates' Courts Service, on which some items in *Part Two* of this handbook are based; and the assistance of Andy Wesson, clerk to the South Bedfordshire magistrates' courts, by reading and commenting on the proofs.

Introduction to the

Family Proceedings Court

Elaine Laken
Chris Bazell
Winston Gordon

Foreword by Sir Stephen Brown
President of the
Family Division of the High Court

Editor Bryan Gibson

WATERSIDE PRESS
WINCHESTER

The authors

Elaine Laken is Justices' Clerk for North Avon and chair of the Family Law Committee of the Justices' Clerks' Society. She is a regular trainer of magistrates and court staff and approved by the Law Society to run courses for solicitors wishing to join the Children Panel. She is a barrister and a member of the National Council for Family Proceedings.

Chris Bazell is Justices' Clerk for Banbury, Bicester and Witney and joint Training Officer for Berkshire and Oxfordshire. A solicitor, he is a former chair of the Justices' Clerks' Society Family Law Committee and Legal Advisor to the Magistrates' Association Family Proceedings Committee. From 1994 to 1997 he was a member of the Children Act Advisory Committee.

Winston Gordon is Justices' Clerk, Justices' Chief Executive and Training Officer for Tameside, Greater Manchester. He is a member of the Executive Committee of the Justices' Clerks' Society Standing Committee of Magistrates' Training Officers and of the Duchy of Lancaster Branch Training Committee. He is a solicitor—with experience of advocacy—a tutor at Continuing Professional Development courses and co-author of *The Sentence of the Court* and *Introduction to the Youth Court*.

Editor

Bryan Gibson is Managing Editor of Waterside Press.

Introduction to the
Family Proceedings Court

CONTENTS

Foreword *vii*

PART ONE

1 Introduction *9*
2 Children *20*
3 Procedures *37*
4 Welfare of the Child *56*
5 Financial Provision *71*
6 Enforcement *85*
7 Domestic Violence and Occupation Orders *99*
8 Adoption *119*

PART TWO

Materials: see overleaf

PART TWO: Materials

A Application Form: Children Act 1989 (and Supplement for Care or Supervision Order) *135*

B Specimen Directions *142*

C Best Practice Notes
  • *For the Judiciary and Family Proceedings Courts When Ordering a Welfare Report (and Pro Forma) 146*
  • *To Court Staff When Welfare Reports Have Been Ordered 150*

D Form to Accompany Direction to Investigate under Section 37 Children Act 1989 *151*

E Definitions: Family Proceedings; Specified Proceedings *153*

F Decision Making *156*

G Findings of Fact and Reasons *160*

H Guide to Lawyers on How to Prepare for Trial *163*

I Experts: Role and Court Expectations *164*

J Specimen Form of Undertaking *166*

Index *168*

Foreword

Sir Stephen Brown

President of the Family Division of the High Court

The passing of the Children Act in 1989 introduced a wholly new dimension to the work of magistrates' courts. The justices who constitute the Family Proceedings Courts are members of specialist panels. They undergo extensive and continuing training in preparation for the important and demanding work which they undertake.

The Justices' Clerks' Society has produced a clear and comprehensive introduction to the law and practice of the Family Proceedings Court. It is a first class work which provides an invaluable framework for panel members and a reference point for all those who are engaged in this important work.

Aims and Objectives

This handbook was compiled under the auspices of the Justices' Clerks' Society by three experienced training officers to magistrates. The intention is:

- to provide a companion for new members of the family panel as they undertake their training and an accessible reference point for experienced magistrates

- to assist trainers by allowing them to concentrate on imparting skills necessary for making informed, balanced and structured decisions—in the knowledge that background material can be found in the handbook

- to inform other court users and students about relevant procedures and requirements, and about how decisions are approached in the family proceedings court

- to produce a lucid account, avoiding jargon and complexity. Items are dealt with in outline only—and further advice should be sought by people who require a more detailed explanation. In particular, when dealing with cases in court, *family panel magistrates should seek the advice of the court legal advisor in all but the most straightforward situations*. This applies with even greater force to family matters than to criminal cases.

PART ONE

1 Introduction *9*

2 Children *20*

3 Procedures *37*

4 Welfare of the Child *56*

5 Financial Provision *71*

6 Enforcement *85*

7 Domestic Violence and Occupation Orders *99*

8 Adoption *119*

CHAPTER 1

Introduction

This handbook provides an outline of the powers and duties of the present-day family proceedings court and deals with all the main aspects of this highly important jurisdiction.

Magistrates' courts have dealt with disputes arising from marriages and certain other family problems for many years. This part of their responsibilities has, over the years, depended on a variety of Acts of Parliament—such as one, only recently repealed, dating back to 1576 under which they could order a father to pay maintenance for the upkeep of an illegitimate child. Similarly, magistrates long had powers to order what used to be 'custody' of and 'access' to children until these concepts were superseded by the fresh approach contained in the Children Act 1989 and described in this work.

Since 1991, magistrates have played an increasingly significant part in the system of family courts (see next section). Apart from divorce cases and rulings affecting rights to property—which are reserved to other courts in the hierarchy—magistrates share in a wide-ranging jurisdiction to deal with family matters, including legal proceedings affecting the lives of children. In some instances, magistrates have exclusive powers as with emergency protection orders (*Chapter 2*) and orders for financial provision between people who remain married (*Chapter 5*). Whatever these powers, they are underpinned by a distinct approach to decision-making which differs markedly from that in criminal cases.

THE SYSTEM OF FAMILY COURTS

The modern-day system of family courts was introduced by the Children Act 1989. Under this system, the following courts deal with family matters:

- the family proceedings court. This is the name given to the magistrates' court when members of the family panel sit to hear this type of case
- the county court. There are a number of 'different' county courts as far as family proceedings are concerned. Some have no family jurisdiction at all. Those which do, always have jurisdiction to deal with divorce, but also fall into one of three categories:

—county courts which only have a divorce jurisdiction

—family hearing centres. These county courts can, in addition to divorce cases, hear contested *private law* cases (see below) and adoption applications

—care centres. These county courts can hear *all* family matters including *public law* cases (see below)

- the High Court of Justice—normally the Family Division.

Apart from aspects of the new shared jurisdiction affecting children, the family proceedings court gathered up existing domestic proceedings (as they were then called) and cases involving the care of children by local authorities (which used to be dealt with by the then juvenile court). It operates under the administrative umbrella of the magistrates' court and in many instances has a 'first-stop' role within the network of courts described above.

Magistrates have only specialised in this type of work in modern times. 'Domestic court panels', the forerunner of 'family panels', only came into being as late as 1979. Before that, such matters were dealt with by the 'ordinary' magistrates' court. Even today, a limited range of family matters can be dealt with in this way *or* in the family proceedings court, for example proceedings to enforce or vary an order for periodical payments (see *Chapter 6*). However, in most areas of the country, all such proceedings are deemed to be more appropriately dealt with by specially trained magistrates in the expert environment of the family proceedings court.

JURISDICTION

The Children Act 1989 repealed and replaced the old law affecting children and now embraces most of the statute law affecting their care and upbringing. The Act also deals with the services which must be provided for children by local authorities. It has revolutionised the law affecting child issues, whether in divorce, family or care proceedings.

Beyond the 1989 Act, magistrates continue to have quite separate powers to make maintenance orders between spouses (*Chapter 5*), to protect them from one another and—once the Family Law Act 1996 is in force—to protect 'associated persons' and to regulate occupation of the family home (*Chapter 7*). Different statutes may need to be considered depending upon the nature of the case. The main provisions affecting law and procedure in the family proceedings court are the:

- Domestic Proceedings and Magistrates' Courts Act 1978
- Magistrates' Courts Act 1980

- Children Act 1989
- Family Law Act 1996.

These statutes are supplemented by extensive rules and regulations. Where appropriate, a note about the effect of these secondary provisions is included in the text of this work. Case law developed by judges of the High Court assists interpretation and application of the provisions. To this must be added a number of Best Practice guides to decision-making or procedures. Examples appear in *Part Two* of this handbook.

Public law and private law cases

The family proceedings court plays a key role in what are termed:

- *public law* cases (e.g. applications for care or supervision orders in respect of children, usually brought by local authorities); and
- *private law* cases (e.g. disputes between parents concerning the upbringing of children).

In 1995, family proceedings courts dealt with 34 per cent of *private law* cases and 85 per cent of *public law* cases involving children. The court also deals with a variety of other matters, including:

- **applications by spouses for financial provision for themselves** i.e. provision for parties who remain married and which falls short of the kind of settlement which can occur on divorce. Associated maintenance arrangements for children—once the province of magistrates—are now for the most part dealt with by the Child Support Agency (CSA). Magistrates still have an enforcement role if the CSA applies for a 'liability order'
- **family protection orders** to prevent domestic violence, and involving, where appropriate, the use of powers to arrest*
- **exclusion orders** to keep a spouse out of the family home and also involving, where appropriate, the use of powers to arrest*
- **emergency protection orders** to deal with any immediate threat to a child
- **supervision orders** in care proceedings courts can make a supervision order in respect of any child under the age of 17. This order will be managed by the local authority in most cases, but that authority can ask the probation service (which also operates a Court Welfare Service) to do this if that service has been involved with the family
- **family assistance orders** designed to assist families through a difficult transition

11

- **enforcement** concerning, for example
  - —Children Act cases; and
  - —orders for financial provision for spouses. Also included under this head is the enforcement of assessments made by the CSA (above), and of maintenance orders from abroad and vice versa (known as 'reciprocal enforcement')
- **adoption** i.e. orders giving parental rights and duties in respect of a child to adoptive parents.

* The law will change when Part IV of the Family Law Act 1996 is in force. 'Non-molestation' and 'occupation' orders—the equivalent of which are currently available through the High Court or county court—will become available generally and be subject to a new uniform code applicable to all tiers of court dealing with family matters (*Chapter 7*).

Other features of the family jurisdiction
The way in which family proceedings courts operate is quite different from the way criminal courts do and requires a fresh 'mind-set'. An aim is to remove conflict and to get away from legal issues in favour of practical solutions. This approach involves, for example:

- a less adversarial approach than in criminal proceedings
- an investigative role for judges and magistrates
- relaxed rules governing evidence and procedure
- liaison between the various courts in the hierarchy
- extensive co-operation between courts and other agencies.

There is also an emphasis on keeping matters 'out of court' and resolving issues by informal methods such as mediation and conciliation. A duty is cast on legal representatives and other practitioners to encourage reconciliation. There is a system of directions hearings whereby many items are dealt with before a case reaches the court proper, and procedures for the exchange of key information in advance of the hearing. These and similar matters are dealt with at appropriate points in this handbook.

CONSTITUTION

Family proceedings courts must be made up of three magistrates from the family panel (below)—and include a man and a woman, unless this is impracticable. Normally, members of the family panel are lay magistrates, i.e. unpaid and not possessing legal qualifications. They are advised by a justices' clerk or other court legal advisor (see *The Role of the*

Justices' Clerk, below). A family proceedings court may comprise a stipendiary magistrate as chairman and one or two lay justices who are members of the family panel. If this is not practicable, the stipendiary magistrate may sit alone.

FAMILY PANELS

Family panels are made up of magistrates selected by their local colleagues for this work on the basis of their aptitude and personal suitability. In addition to their special duties in the family proceedings court, members of the panel continue to serve in the ordinary magistrates' court (except in London where special arrangements exist for members to be appointed direct to the panel).

Magistrates serve on the panel for a three year term. New panels came into being on 1 January 1997. Existing members are eligible for re-election when a new panel is formed. The whole bench must decide how many magistrates need to be on the panel having regard to the amount of work in their area, and which of its members to appoint. When deciding upon the number, the Lord Chancellor has indicated that the bench should bear in mind that each panel member needs to sit at least 12 times a year in order to stay in touch and gain experience. In some rural areas difficulties arise in trying to ensure not only that all members reach this level of sittings, but also that there are enough members for family proceedings courts to sit at short notice to deal with urgent applications. In some areas of the country these problems have been overcome by panels from adjoining areas combining.

Chairmen and deputy chairmen
The panel appoints its own chairman. It also selects enough deputy court chairmen to ensure that family proceedings courts are always chaired by someone trained for this role. Before any magistrate can chair a family proceedings court, he or she must undergo Chairmanship Training. This must be repeated every six years.

TRAINING

When magistrates join the family panel they receive specialist guidance and support. Previous experience of criminal proceedings and a limited range of everyday civil matters (such as the enforcement of unpaid council tax) is small preparation for making complex and far-reaching decisions about children, family finances or domestic violence. There are thus special training courses. Training starts with a Foundation

Programme, normally of about 12 hours duration which must be completed before a new member of the panel sits in court to hear cases. This is followed by a Basic Training Programme involving a further eight hours of training which has to be completed between six and 18 months after the new member first adjudicates. Experienced panel members have to undertake Refresher Training of at least 12 hours in every three years. The Judicial Studies Board advises magistrates' courts committees and training officers on the syllabus for these courses. It suggests that the Foundation Course should be designed to equip magistrates to:

- apply their knowledge of the underlying principles of the Children Act 1989, in particular those key tenets of the Act explained in *Chapter 2* of this handbook, i.e. that:
  —the welfare of the child is paramount
  —delay is normally harmful
  —the court should only intervene by making orders in respect of children if to do so is better for the child than making no order
- use the range of powers available to achieve the best outcome for the child
- know of the powers available to deal with financial orders (*Chapter 5*) and domestic violence (*Chapter 7*)
- use appropriate procedures and practice when dealing with families (as explained at appropriate points throughout this work)
- appreciate the role of the different parties, agencies and officers in family proceedings such as the local authority, guardian ad litem and welfare officer (see, particularly, *Chapters 2* and *4*)
- adopt a structured approach to decision-making (see *Part Two* of this handbook) and apply the welfare checklist (*Chapter 2*) when appropriate
- contribute to the process of formulating reasons for decisions.

'Depth of knowledge' and openness
Lord Mackay of Clashfern, when Lord Chancellor, pointed out:

this is not an area where a knowledge of the black letters of the law takes one very far . . . Especially where local authorities are involved, and in cases of child abuse, those concerned in proceedings need to have a special depth of knowledge of relevant matters going far beyond the law. They need to be versed in local authority and social work practice and to know what can be achieved for children by that route. They need to be familiar with some aspects of medical and psychiatric practice. In addition, they may also need to come to terms with strong personal feelings and to have mastered them before they participate in cases involving child abuse.

Another training need identified by the Family Proceedings Committee of the Magistrates' Association concerns assessing evidence from expert witnesses, a concern repeated in guidance issued by the Magisterial Committee of the Judicial Studies Board. A relevant training pack was launched in 1994: 'The Welfare of the Child: Assessing Evidence in Children Cases'. This pioneered a fresh approach in that course material is delivered via a mix of self-study and group sessions. The pack consists of six 'work books' which introduce a range of topics, including the developmental needs of children, and the range of services available to children and families.

Training also seeks to ensure a culture within family proceedings courts based on openness by all concerned, including the court. In most other contexts magistrates are expected to keep their deliberations private, but in the family proceedings court they must communicate openly and, in many situations, have a legal duty—assisted by a legal advisor—to explain their decisions. The skills involved include the ability to handle large volumes of information, much of which is in written form. Family panel magistrates (and other practitioners) need to prepare *before* going into court by reading case documents and identifying issues. As already indicated, the approach is more inquisitorial than magistrates will have been used to, and often means asking questions to clarify points, or 'fill in gaps' as the case proceeds.

ROLE OF THE JUSTICES' CLERK

The justices' clerk has the following functions in relation to family proceedings:

- legal advisor
- case manager
- collecting officer.

Certain of these responsibilities may be carried out by other court legal advisors who, in some instances, must be specifically authorised.

Legal advice
Fundamentally speaking, the duty of the justices' clerk or other court legal advisor to advise magistrates on law, practice, procedure and evidence is the same as in relation to criminal proceedings. A fuller account is contained in *The Sentence of the Court: A Handbook for Magistrates* (Waterside Press, 1995). However, certain important differences must be emphasised.

The statutory rules require that in the family proceedings court the advisor records the magistrates' findings of fact and drafts their reasons. This, in effect, demands that he or she is with the magistrates during their private discussions. Obviously, he or she must be meticulous not to steer the discussion in any particular direction, except to the extent of ensuring a correct legal approach to issues of fact or law.

Case management
The key procedures affecting the control of cases are known as 'allocations' and 'directions'. The allocation of cases to a given court is initially a matter for the justices' clerk. The principles upon which he or she will act are explained in *Chapter 3*. However, the parties can seek a review of the allocation decision by the court, or ask at a court hearing for the case to be transferred elsewhere.

Directions appointments are regularly held in advance of a court hearing to deal with preliminary items. They are normally held in private. Directions can be given by the justices' clerk, a member of the panel or the court. In practice, at the pre-hearing stage they are often given by the justices' clerk or an authorised legal advisor. Where the need for the direction occurs during the course of a court hearing, the court itself will often deal with the matter. Usually, the parties to the case, their legal representatives and other people concerned will attend. The justices' clerk will try to establish among things:

- what issues are in dispute, if any
- whether there is any measure of agreement
- whether there is a prospect of agreement being reached without the continued involvement of the court
- what information or evidence needs to be obtained or exchanged
- whether, in a case involving a child, a guardian ad litem or solicitor needs to be appointed to represent the child
- an appropriate timetable.

The justices' clerk as collecting officer
The justices' clerk is responsible in his or her role as the court 'collecting officer' for the receipt and payment of money arriving at the court in response to orders for financial provision: see, generally, *Chapter 5*. Enforcement of such orders also takes place in the name of the collecting officer. 'Collecting office' is the name given to that part of the court administration which deals with the collection and transmission of such payments and which usually deals with family court process, for example applications to start proceedings. It is possible for the collecting office function for several courts to be centralised under one justices' clerk (and for this one aspect of his or her responsibilities to be held

jointly with or conferred separately on the justices' chief executive for the area).

LEGAL REPRESENTATION

The Law Society has established a Children Panel for solicitors wishing to act for children in family courts. Although not yet compulsory, in practice in *public law* cases the legal representatives of all parties are invariably drawn from the panel.

Membership is open only to solicitors in private practice. Applicants must demonstrate experience of representing children in proceedings under the Children Act 1989 or show relevant advocacy experience and knowledge of procedures gained by representing parents, grand-parents or other parties in *public law* and *private law* contested proceedings. They must also be able to demonstrate knowledge of procedures gained by observing at least one contested local authority case—where the child is represented—no earlier than 12 months prior to the date of application for membership.

Applicants must have practised for at least three years and have attended two one-day approved courses, one on law and procedure and the other on skills and practices, again not earlier than 12 months prior to the application. Certain undertakings are required and references may be sought. The solicitor is required to attend for interview and submit written answers to a case study and questions on working with children. Successful applicants are appointed for a five year term and a certificate of membership is issued. After five years, they must apply for re-appointment.

In care proceedings (*Chapter 2*), all parents and children are entitled to free legal aid irrespective of their financial circumstances or the merits of the case.

ADVISORY BOARD ON FAMILY LAW

A Children Act Advisory Committee was set up in 1991 to monitor the operation of the Children Act 1989 and to comment on issues arising from its implementation. From July 1997, that committee is replaced by the Advisory Board in Family Law. This is an inter-disciplinary board and one of its terms of reference is:

... to maintain an overview of the working of the policies embodied in the Children Act within the family court system.

A network of Family Court Business Committees and Family Court Forums (see below) continues to deal with operational aspects of Children Act work at local level. They are able to refer policy issues to the Lord Chancellor, the Court Service, relevant government departments or the board itself.

FAMILY COURT BUSINESS COMMITTEES

Family court business committees operate throughout England and Wales from each county court care centre. They examine the process of litigation and court procedures under the Children Act 1989 to ensure that cases are managed efficiently and effectively, having regard to the resources available. Committees are required to:

- ensure that arrangements are working properly at local level, particularly in relation to the allocation and transfer of cases, and that agreed targets are met, where appropriate
- seek to achieve administrative consistency between the three tiers of court: the High Court, county court and family proceedings court
- ensure that guardians ad litem and court welfare services (*Chapter 4*) are aware of the needs of the family courts, and that courts avoid making unreasonable demands on these services
- liaise with the family court forum for the area (below)
- standardise practice where more than one local authority is involved.

Family Court Business Committees are chaired by a designated family judge and membership is drawn from courts, agencies and disciplines whose practice, procedures and policies have a direct impact on family proceedings. Topics examined by local committees include:

- explanation of orders to children
- delay in producing court welfare reports
- the use of directions to the parties to proceedings (*Chapter 3*).

FAMILY COURT FORUMS

These came into effect in 1994. The aim is for representatives of regular family court practitioners to have a flexible meeting under the following terms of reference:

- to promote discussion and encourage co-operation between all the professions, agencies and organizations involved in or concerned with family proceedings and to provide occasions for this to occur at each county court care centre
- to consider issues which arise locally in the conduct of family proceedings with particular reference to the practice of the:
  - —courts
  - —legal profession
  - —probation service
  - —medical profession
  - —health authorities
  - —social services
  - —education authorities; and
  - —police (family matters may overlap with criminal acts, e.g. child abuse or assault)
- to recommend action which can be taken locally to improve the service provided to the parties to family proceedings
- to consider whether special events, seminars, study days or conferences are required in addition to routine meetings to disseminate good practice, new arrangements and ideas, or to examine problems.

Sessions have taken place, for example, on subjects such as child protection, the use of expert witnesses, the effect of the 1989 Act on police investigations, children's mental health, the inter-relationship between care and criminal proceedings, and the feelings and wishes of children.

COURT USER GROUPS

Many magistrates' courts have local user groups where the administration of the court is discussed with other practitioners who work locally—including family court specialists. In some court areas there is a large enough family proceedings workload for there to be a specialist user group devoted exclusively to this type of work, or for a sub-committee of the main user group to be formed to deal with family matters. User groups provide a focus for resolving local issues.

CHAPTER 2

Children

Dealing with applications under the Children Act 1989 is one of the most important aspects of the work of the family panel. The 1989 Act replaced a large part of the existing, fragmented law concerning disputes over children, consolidating and simplifying it, and stressing:

- the notion of 'parental responsibility'
- the wishes, feelings and needs of children
- the idea that no order at all should be made unless it is in the child's best interests to make an order; and
- an investigative as opposed to an adversarial approach.

The former terms 'custody' (i.e. of children) and 'access' (to children by a parent) were superseded and replaced by four new concepts: 'contact', 'residence', 'specific issues' and 'prohibited steps'. A new, short term order known as a 'family assistance order' was also introduced. These and other measures designed to protect children and safeguard their welfare—including the powers of local authorities to seek to intervene in the care and supervision of children—are explained in the course of this chapter.

WELFARE OF THE CHILD

In relation to *all* decisions affecting children, the court must observe the welfare principle and associated rules designed to ensure that its actions and decisions serve the best interests of the child. This is the subject matter of *Chapter 4*.

PARENTAL RESPONSIBILITY

The Children Act 1989 works through the idea of 'parental responsibility', which embraces all the rights, powers and duties of a parent in relation to a child and his or her property. For the present, it is sufficient to note that the exercise of parental responsibility can be controlled by the court by means of what are universally known as 'section 8 orders', and that if a care order is made in favour of a local authority, the authority will acquire parental responsibility to run alongside that of the child's parents. Further information about parental responsibility is given under the heading *The New Model of Parenthood* later in this chapter.

SECTION 8 ORDERS

Whenever a court is dealing with *any* application which falls within the definition of 'family proceedings' (*Chapter 3*) the court can consider making section 8 orders. These are also the main types of *private law* application. The court can make section 8 orders *on application* by an individual or *of its own motion*. Certain people are entitled to apply for a section 8 order, for example a parent or anyone with a residence order in their favour in relation to the child. Other people must ask the court for leave to apply—when it will consider criteria set out in the 1989 Act: see p. 22. The High Court will only grant leave to a child if satisfied that he or she 'has sufficient understanding to make the proposed application'.

- *contact orders* these require someone with whom a child lives, or is to live, to allow the child to be visited by, or to visit or stay with, someone else—or for there to be some form of remote contact with the child, for example by telephone or letter (sometimes called 'indirect contact')
- *residence orders* these determine where a child will live and who the child is to live with. Whilst stability for the child is a highly important factor, different arrangements can be ordered in respect of different periods and these may involve different people. A residence order confers parental responsibility. However, certain items require the consent of more than one person
- *specific issues orders* here the court gives directions to settle individual questions which have arisen, or may arise, in relation to the child. Orders require someone with parental responsibility to act in a particular way, for example concerning the child's health or education
- *prohibited steps orders* these prevent something—which could have been done by a parent in carrying out his or her parental responsibility—from happening without the consent of the court, for example a medical operation or removal of the child from the United Kingdom.

Section 8 orders: restrictions
There are a number of restrictions contained in section 9 of the 1989 Act which should be noted:

- of the four orders listed, only a residence order can be made in relation to a child who is already in the care of a local authority. The residence order then operates to discharge the existing care order
- a local authority is barred from applying for either a residence order or a contact order
- neither can a court make a specific issue or prohibited steps order in favour of a local authority in order to achieve a result similar to that which would have been achieved by making a residence or contact order. In one appeal case, a local authority applied for a prohibited steps order—the terms of which stopped a father seeing his child or living in the child's home. The court held that this was the same result that would have been achieved by making a contact or residence order and that the local authority could not circumvent the prohibition in this way. Local authorities can obtain such orders if for *bona fide* reasons
- a foster-parent appointed by a local authority cannot obtain leave to apply for a section 8 order unless he or she has the consent of that authority, or is a relative of the child, or the child has lived with him or her for at least three years within the five years immediately preceding the application.

Who can apply for a section 8 order?

Apart from the restrictions noted under the previous heading, the 1989 Act allows virtually anyone to apply for a section 8 order. However, with the exception of parents and guardians, most applicants need to obtain leave before an application can proceed and this would obviously not be given to someone without a legitimate interest. The following criteria must be taken into account:

- the nature of the proposed application
- the applicant's connection with the child
- the risk of harmful disruption to the child
- where the child is being 'looked after' by the local authority, the authority's plans for the child's future, and the wishes and feelings of the child's parents or guardians.

Case law demands that such applications are carefully considered. Further, if the court feels there is little likelihood of the application succeeding then leave should be refused.

FAMILY ASSISTANCE ORDERS

Under section 16 Children Act 1989, where the court has power to make a section 8 order—i.e. in any 'family proceedings' (see the definition of that term in *Part Two* of this handbook)—it can make a family assistance order (often referred to as an 'FAO'). This power exists whether or not the court makes any other order.

A family assistance order requires a social worker or court welfare officer (*Chapter 4*) to advise, assist and befriend the people named in the order. Those people can be the parent, the child, and anyone with whom the child is living or in whose favour a contact order is in force. A family assistance order can last for up to six months. There are two statutory constraints:

- the circumstances must be 'exceptional'; and
- each individual named in the order must consent (except the child).

The statistics show that these orders are quite rarely made.

CARE ORDERS AND SUPERVISION ORDERS

Care proceedings are amongst the most difficult any family panel magistrate is called upon to take part in. When informal mechanisms and partnership with parents on a voluntary, non-statutory basis break down or are inappropriate, Part IV of the Children Act 1989 allows the local authority or the NSPCC to bring care proceedings.

Threshold criteria
A court can only make a care order (or supervision order: below) if satisfied:

(a) that the child concerned is suffering, or is likely to suffer, significant harm; and
(b) that the harm, or likelihood of harm, is attributable to:
the care given to the child, or likely to be given to him if the order were not made, not being what it would be reasonable to expect a parent to give him;
or the child being beyond parental control.

These are the 'threshold criteria' (sometimes called 'grounds'). They do not in themselves justify a care or supervision order, but are simply a basis for this, the minimum requirement before the court can go on to consider whether, in all the circumstances, it ought to make an order.

The court must, in particular, have regard to the welfare principle in section 1 of the 1989 Act (*Chapter 4*) and the principle of 'no order' under which it may be better to leave matters as they stand with the child still at home under the care and supervision of his or her parents.

'Significant harm'
The criteria use the term 'significant harm'. Mere harm is not enough. Harm is defined as ill-treatment or impairment of health or development (concepts then further defined to include, for example, sexual abuse, emotional abuse and neglect). The Act does not define the word 'significant' but case law indicates that the ordinary dictionary definition applies. Further, when

> ... the question of whether harm suffered by a child is significant turns on the child's health or development, his health or development shall be compared with that which could reasonably be expected of a similar child.

Not only must 'significant harm', or its likelihood, be established, but also that the harm is attributable to a failure of reasonable parental care or that the child is beyond parental control.

Plans for the child
The local authority will also need to tell the court about its own plans for the child if an order were to be made. This will be relevant to the child's welfare and whether an order should be made. In relation to contact by people with the child, before making a care order the court must:
—consider the arrangements the authority has made, or proposes to make, for affording any individual contact with the child; and
—invite the parties to comment on those arrangements.

Effect of a care order on parental responsibility
When a care order is made the natural parents continue to have parental responsibility for the child in question. The authority acquire parental responsibility, but share this with the parents. Simply because parents are not physically looking after their children, this does not mean that they have lost responsibility for them, or any say in the matter. The authority can only limit the exercise of rights by parents if necessary to safeguard and promote the welfare of the child, or to the extent that this has been ordered by a court. One purpose is to reduce the likelihood of disputes with parents and to promote partnership.

Supervision orders

Subject to the same threshold criteria set out above, the court can make an order placing a child under the supervision of the local authority or a probation officer. Most orders are supervised by local authority social workers. A child may only be placed under the supervision of a probation officer if the local authority so request and a probation officer is already exercising, or has exercised, in relation to another member of the household, duties imposed on it by statute (the Probation Service also provides a Court Welfare Service: *Chapter 4*). The duty of the supervising officer is to:

- advise, assist and befriend the child
- take such steps as are reasonably necessary to give effect to the order; and
- where the order is not wholly complied with, or the officer thinks it is no longer necessary, to consider applying for a variation or discharge.

Duration of care orders

Care orders:

- can only be obtained in relation to people under 17 years of age (or 16 if married)
- continue in force until the child reaches 18 years unless brought to an end sooner by another court order.

A residence order also acts to discharge any existing care order: above.

Duration of supervision orders

Supervision orders:

- can only be obtained in relation to people under 17 years of age (or 16 if married)
- can be made for up to 12 months to start with. The supervising officer can apply for an extension or extensions for up to three years from the date of the original order
- in any event
  —cease when a child attains the age of 18; or
  —if brought to an end by another court order.

EDUCATION SUPERVISION ORDERS (ESOs)

Truancy is not in itself a ground for a care or supervision order. However, in some instances the facts surrounding failure to attend school may fall within the threshold criteria for a care or supervision order, i.e. because of what the child was doing whilst truanting. Section 36 of the 1989 Act makes special provision for education supervision orders where a child is of compulsory school age and not being properly educated. These are *not* specified proceedings, so that no guardian ad litem can be appointed.

In practice, ESOs are managed by the local education authority, usually through its education welfare service. The supervisor is under a duty to advise, assist and befriend and to give directions to the child and his or her parents in such a way as to secure that the child is properly educated. If the child fails to comply with the ESO, the local education authority must notify the local authority, which then has to investigate the child's circumstances—or, on discharging the order, the court can direct this. A parent who persistently fails to comply with a direction under an ESO commits a criminal offence punishable in the magistrates' court by a Level 3 fine (i.e. up to £1,000. May, 1997).

INTERIM ORDERS AND SHORT TERM ORDERS

The progress of cases is linked to the principle that delay works against the interests of the child (*Chapter 4*). Whilst directions appointments are designed to bring cases speedily to a conclusion, there are many reasons why a court cannot make or consider a final order. Powers then exist to make interim orders or short term orders as described below.

Private law cases
During an adjournment of a section 8 case the court can make any short term order such as a residence or contact order.

Public law cases
There is power in care proceedings to make an interim care order or an interim supervision order if:

- the proceedings are adjourned; or
- the court gives a direction under section 37 of the 1989 Act for the local authority to investigate the child's situation: below.

The court can only make an interim order if satisfied that there are *reasonable grounds for believing* that the threshold criteria are met (see under the heading *Care Orders and Supervision Orders* above).

Number and duration of interim care orders or supervision orders

There is no limit to the number of interim orders a court can make before the matter comes to a full hearing. However, there *is* a limit on their length. The general rule is that no interim care or supervision order can last for more than *four weeks*, but there is a special *eight week* limit when a court makes an interim order for the first time, beginning on the day that it makes the order. Within these limits, the order can be of any length.

The eight week period could be 'filled up' by a single order or a series of short orders lasting for a total of eight weeks. If, towards the end of eight weeks, a court wishes to make an interim order which will overrun that period, the four week rule applies to that order and any subsequent order sought. The following provisions should be noted:

- the court must draw up a timetable with a view to 'disposing of the application without delay'
- when making an interim order and determining the period for which the order is to be in force, the court must consider whether any party who was, or might have been, opposed to the making of the order was in a position to argue his or her case against the order in full.

A court can, when it makes an interim care or supervision order, give directions concerning medical, psychiatric or other assessment of the child. The House of Lords has ruled that this power can be used to require a local authority to conduct a residential assessment of a child and parent. No medical or other assessment can take place during an interim order without permission from the court.

INVESTIGATIONS BY LOCAL AUTHORITIES

Certain duties to investigate the circumstances of children are cast on local authorities by the 1989 Act. Where a local authority:

(a) is informed that a child who lives, or is found, in their area:
   (i) is the subject of an emergency protection order (see below); or
   (ii) is in police protection; or
(b) have reasonable cause to suspect that a child who lives, or is found, in their area is suffering, or is likely to suffer, significant harm,
the authority shall make, or cause to be made, such enquiries as they consider necessary to enable them to decide whether they should take any action to safeguard or promote the child's welfare (section 47(1)).

The duty is qualified as follows:

Where . . . a local authority conclude that they should take action to safeguard or promote the child's welfare they shall take that action (so far as it is both within their power and reasonably practicable for them to do so) (section 47(8)).

Under section 37 of the 1989 Act, the court can direct such investigations, for example where features of a *private law* application for a section 8 order indicate a need for scrutiny by an authority charged with *public law* responsibilities. The local authority must consider whether they should:

- apply for a care order or a supervision order
- provide services or assistance for the child or his or her family;
- take any other appropriate action with respect to the child.

If the authority decides *not* to apply for a care order or supervision order, they must inform the court of:

- the reasons for this
- any service or assistance which they have provided, or intend to provide; and
- any other action taken or proposed with respect to the child.

This information must normally be given to the court within eight weeks. A suggested form to accompany a direction to a local authority to investigate is contained in *Part Two* of this handbook.

THE NEW MODEL OF PARENTHOOD

The concept of parental responsibility is central to decision-making with regard to children. Rather than concentrating solely on someone's rights as the parent or guardian of a child, there has been a shift towards stressing responsibilities towards the child as part of several incidents of parenthood, i.e. 'rights, duties, powers, responsibilities and authority' (section 3(1) Children Act 1989).

Married parents and all mothers have parental responsibility. Unmarried fathers have to acquire it either through obtaining a court order or by written agreement with the mother. Unmarried fathers and other people can also acquire parental responsibility through a residence order or adoption.

The state (in the guise of the local authority social services department) can only acquire parental responsibility for a child by order of a court. Where it *does* acquire parental responsibility (i.e. via a care order or emergency protection order), the 1989 Act imposes duties to consult with and involve parents in decisions about their children—the 'partnership model'.

Durability of parental responsibility

In the arena of *private law*, the fact of divorce or separation does not in itself affect the parental responsibility of the child's parents. This will continue beyond the marriage, and can only be brought to a complete end by an adoption order or an order freeing the child for adoption: *Chapter 8*. Similarly, if someone acquires parental responsibility (as, e.g. where a residence order is made) responsibility is shared. The 1989 Act states:

> A person who has parental responsibility for a child at any time shall not cease to have that responsibility solely because some other person subsequently acquires parental responsibility for the child. (Section 2(6))

Section 8 orders—discussed earlier in this chapter—involving contact, residence, specific issues or prohibited steps allow for the regulation of parental responsibility on specific matters, but do not fundamentally contradict this fact of continuing parental responsibility. The same applies when a care order is made. The parental responsibility of parents or guardians continues alongside that acquired by the local authority.

Consent of more than one person

Normally, there is a right of independent action on the part of someone with parental responsibility. However, some events in the life of a child normally require the consent of more than one person:

- freeing for adoption and agreement to adoption require consent from each parent: Adoption Act 1976 (*Chapter 8*)
- removal from the United Kingdom requires the consent of each parent: Child Abduction Act 1984
- marriage by someone below the age of 18 years requires the consent of each parent: Marriage Act 1949
- applications by non-parents for residence and contact orders can sometimes require the consent of all people with parental responsibility: section 10 Children Act 1989
- changing a child's name or removing him or her from the United Kingdom for more than a month *when subject to a residence order or care order* needs the consent of all people with parental responsibility: sections 13 and 33 Children Act 1989
- where a child subject to a residence order is provided with accommodation, all people in whose favour the residence order is in force must agree to the child being removed from it: section 20 Children Act 1989.

The duty to consult
In the *public law* field there are several instances where parents and other people must be consulted. If the child is the subject of a care order (when the parents share parental responsibility with the local authority), the authority cannot exercise control unless satisfied that it is necessary to do so to safeguard or promote the child's welfare. A local authority which is 'looking after' a child (including children for whom it is providing accommodation as well as those in care under a court order) is under a duty to find out the wishes and feelings of the following people before making any decision concerning the child:

- the child
- the parents
- any non-parent with parental responsibility (e.g. a grandparent who has been given that responsibility by a court)
- any other people whose wishes and feelings the authority considers relevant (section 22 Children Act 1989).

In contrast, there is *no right* to be consulted in the *private law* sphere where one person with parental responsibility wishes to exercise it—so that it is up to people to make their own arrangements in a responsible manner, with the possibility of court proceedings as a back up. Where a court makes 'no order' (*Chapter 4*) each parent continues to enjoy a right of decision-making in relation to the child. Even where the court makes an order, parental responsibility and hence freedom of decision-making, is only affected to the extent indicated by the order.

Other issues arising from parental responsibility
The co-existence of parental responsibility with rights of independent decision-making mean that certain points require clarification:

Impact of a residence order
Where a residence order is in force, people with parental responsibility but without the benefit of that order are disadvantaged: they cannot object to the child being accommodated by the local authority, nor can they remove the child from such accommodation.

Unmarried fathers

An unmarried father can take steps to have the relationship with his own child legally recognised via the 1989 Act. He can obtain parental responsibility by:

- a court order
- formal agreement with the mother
- obtaining a residence order in his favour (in which event, if the father does not already have parental responsibility for the child, the court must make an order conferring this).

Surviving parent or guardian

On the death of a parent, guardianship does not take effect automatically so as to run alongside the parental responsibility of the surviving parent. Only when that parent dies will it do so. An exception occurs where there is a residence order in favour of the deceased parent, in which case the appointment of a guardian by that parent means that the guardian's parental responsibility takes effect immediately on the death of the parent appointing the guardian. Parental responsibility is then shared between the surviving parent and the guardian.

Children's rights: the Gillick principle

The change of approach heralded by the 1989 Act does not affect the underlying common law in so far as *children's rights* are concerned. With mature children, the 'Gillick principle' (*Gillick v West Norfolk and Wisbech Area Health Authority* [1986] AC 112) limits the authority of parents and other people who step into their shoes. As Lord Mackay of Clashfern, former Lord Chancellor, said during the passing of the 1989 Act:

> This Bill does nothing to change the underlying principle of *Gillick*, which has to be taken into account by all who exercise parental responsibility over a child mature and intelligent enough to take decisions for himself. (Hansard, House of Lords, Vol. 502, Col. 1351)

The approach in the Gillick case—under which children who are mature enough and capable of understanding the implications of their decisions can give or refuse consent—has been embodied in the Act so that, for example, a child *over the age of 16* can consent to being provided with accommodation even when the parents object. It is arguable that at common law *a mature 15-year-old* could give such consent.

Specific rights to refuse consent
Some provision of the 1989 Act give expression to the *Gillick* legacy and confer on children a statutory 'right to refuse' if of sufficient understanding to make an informed decision, i.e. in relation to:

- interim supervision orders or care orders (section 38)
- supervision orders (schedule 3, paragraphs 4 and 5)
- child assessment orders (section 43)
- emergency protection orders (section 44).

CHILD PROTECTION

Quite apart from the powers of local authorities to seek care orders or supervision orders, other varieties of public intervention fall to be considered:

- child assessment orders
- emergency protection orders
- recovery orders
- police protection.

Emergency protection orders and 'police protection' powers are exclusively linked to child protection, whilst child assessment and recovery orders may have that effect.

Child assessment order (CAO) (section 43 Children Act 1989)
The purpose of a child assessment order is to supplement the powers of social workers in organizing an assessment of a child's physical, emotional or psychological well-being. Sometimes, the requirements of an emergency protection order (below) may not be met, but nevertheless there is concern about the child's welfare.

Only the local authority or NSPCC can apply for a CAO. The proceedings are 'on notice' (see *Chapter 3*) and the child will normally be represented by a guardian ad litem. Before it can grant a CAO, the court must be satisfied that:

- the applicant has reasonable cause to suspect that the child is suffering, or is likely to suffer, significant harm
- there is a need for an assessment of the state of the child's health or development, or the way in which he or she has been treated, to enable the applicant to determine whether the child is suffering, or likely to suffer, significant harm (in effect, whether the threshold criteria for a care order are met); and

- it is unlikely that such an assessment will be made, or be satisfactory, in the absence of a CAO.

A CAO requires someone who is in a position to do so to produce the child to an individual named in the order; and to comply with any directions relating to the assessment of the child as the court sees fit to specify. The order:

- authorises assessment in accordance with its terms
- does not permit assessment of a mature child if he or she refuses consent
- only allows a child to be kept away from his or her home in accordance with any directions given by the court in the order and necessary for the purposes of the assessment, for example, attendance at a clinic. If the child *is* to be kept away from home, the order must contain such directions concerning contact with other people as the court sees fit
- does *not* confer parental responsibility
- lasts for a maximum of seven days. This may cause practical problems, but the process of assessment need not start immediately—the provisions allow the order to be made effective from a later date (e.g. when a hospital bed becomes available).

The court will not make a CAO if satisfied that there are grounds for making an emergency protection order (next heading), or that it ought to make an EPO rather than a CAO.

Emergency protection order (EPO) (section 44 Children Act 1989)
An emergency protection order allows immediate compulsory intervention to protect a child, whilst giving the parents or guardians a reasonable opportunity to challenge the basis of the intervention. The EPO:

- is a vital supplement to the investigative duty of the local authority or NSPCC (above), where either is making enquiries and access to the child is being frustrated—but is required as a matter of urgency
- provides a general basis on which the child can be protected from significant harm by being kept at or removed from given surroundings.

An EPO can be obtained by:

- any person if—but only if—the court is satisfied that there is *reasonable cause to believe* that the child is likely to suffer significant harm if:

  —he or she is not removed to accommodation provided by or on behalf of the applicant; or

  —he or she does not remain in the place in which he or she is being accommodated.

  The court must be satisfied that there is *reasonable cause to believe* that the child is likely to suffer significant harm. Subject to this, the provision would cover the situation where, for example, a child is in hospital and the applicant wants to prevent his or her removal by a parent.

- a local authority or the NSPCC if the court is satisfied that:

  —enquiries are being made with respect to the child; and

  —they are being frustrated by access to the child being unreasonably refused; and

  —the applicant, being someone entitled to seek access, has *reasonable cause to believe* that this is required as a matter of urgency.

Key features of the EPO

The order requires any person who is in a position to do so to produce the child if so requested. It authorises the removal of the child to accommodation provided by the applicant, but only in order to safeguard the child's welfare. The applicant is under a duty to return the child home if it is safe to do so. The local authority has power to assist an alleged perpetrator of child abuse to obtain alternative accommodation. (When the Family Law Act 1996 is in force, the court will have power to order the abuser to leave the home: *Chapter 7*). Where applicable, the EPO prevents the child from being removed from a hospital or other place in which he or she is being accommodated immediately before the making of the order to safeguard his or her welfare. There is a presumption the applicant will allow the child reasonable contact with:

- parents
- people with parental responsibility
- people with whom the child was living immediately before the order was made
- people with the benefit of an existing contact order
- anyone awarded contact by the EPO; and
- people acting on behalf of any of the above.

The presumption is subject to any directions by the court. The court also has power to:

34

- give directions with respect to medical or psychiatric examination or other assessment of the child. As with a CAO, a mature child is legally entitled, if of sufficient understanding to make an informed decision, to refuse to submit to examination or assessment
- strengthen the EPO by requiring someone to disclose any information concerning the child's whereabouts, or by permitting the applicant to enter premises to search for the child (or another child).

The court may issue a warrant—authorising police assistance and the use of reasonable force—where it appears that:

- someone attempting to exercise powers under an EPO has been prevented from doing so by being refused entry to the premises or access to the child concerned; or
- that any such person is likely to be so prevented from exercising any such powers.

Duration of emergency protection orders
An EPO can last for up to eight days (although it can be challenged after 72 hours). There can be just *one* application for an extension for a further seven days. An extension can only be granted if the court has *reasonable cause to believe* that the child is likely to suffer significant harm if the order is not extended. Only a local authority or the NSPCC can apply for the extension.

'Emergency nature' of the order
A consequence of obtaining an EPO is that local authorities or lawyers representing parents and children may have to act immediately or to mount a challenge after 72 hours. Among other things, social workers need to notify the local authority legal department *as soon as* an EPO has been obtained, if they have not already done so. Even with a full seven day EPO plus an extension, this means that if, by day 15, the authority is still concerned about the child it will usually need to apply for an interim care order. It will then have to establish that there are reasonable grounds for believing that the 'threshold criteria' for a care order are met.

Recovery order (RO) (section 50 Children Act 1989)
Where a child subject to a care order absconds or is abducted, the local authority or NSPCC may apply to the family proceedings court for a recovery order. The court can grant the order if it is satisfied that there is reason to believe that the child:

- has been unlawfully taken away or is being unlawfully kept away from the responsible person
- has run away or is staying away from the responsible person
- is missing.

The order authorises the removal of the child by the person authorised by the court, normally any constable or authorised officer of the local authority. The order also operates as a direction to any person who is in a position to do so to produce the child on request to the authorised person.

Police protection (section 46 Children Act 1989)
The Act gives a police constable power to remove a child to suitable accommodation and to keep him or her there, or take reasonable steps to ensure that a child's removal from hospital or some other place in which he or she is being accommodated is prevented. The officer must have reasonable cause to believe that the child would otherwise be likely to suffer significant harm. The child may be kept in police protection for 72 hours. Detention for a longer period may—and only can—be authorised by way of an emergency protection order, failing which the child must be released.

VARIATION AND DISCHARGE OF ORDERS

Courts always have power to discharge or vary an order when this is applied for, and in some situations of their own motion.

CHAPTER 3

Procedures

An understanding of certain procedures is essential to comprehending how the family proceedings court functions. This chapter provides an outline of what, in its more detailed aspects, is the province of justices' clerks, court legal advisors, Children Panel lawyers and other professionals. It focuses on:

- confidentiality
- statutory rules and requirements
- how applications are made
- who the parties are
- service of documents
- directions
- seeing a child 'in private'
- court hearings (including some points about evidence)
- fact finding and reasons for decisions
- duties of legal representatives
- experts
- costs
- appeals.

Most applications to the family proceedings court fall within the ambit of the Children Act 1989 and its associated rules of procedure. These apply to all matters within the definition of 'family proceedings' set out in *Part Two* of this handbook. This chapter deals with these and other 'general' procedures. More specialised rules—like those governing emergency applications or financial support—are covered within the chapters dealing with those topics.

CONFIDENTIALITY

Modern-day rules continue the longstanding prohibition on the public attending family proceedings. Basically, this means that only parties, practitioners and court personnel can attend—and, for example, *bona fide* students or researchers if the court grants leave. Members of the press can attend but publication is so restricted that this is almost defunct. Similarly, no outsider has any right to see forms, statements and other documents, only:

- the court (i.e. magistrates and court officials)
- the parties and their legal advisors; and
- any guardian ad litem or court welfare officer.

The leave of the court is required if someone wishes to disclose information to a third party. The Children Act Advisory Committee stated that lawyers should not normally send family proceedings documents to clients, but ought to insist on the client reading these at their office. Since 1995, any party can apply to keep their *own address* confidential. If the court agrees, it will not then disclose it to other parties in the absence of a successful application to do so.

STATUTORY RULES

Procedure is governed by the Family Proceedings Court (Children Act 1989) Rules 1991 (referred to in this handbook as 'the FPC rules'). Comparable rules exist in relation to the High Court and county court, the main differences in the FPC rules reflecting the role of the justices' clerk. The rules reinforce the shift away from adversarial proceedings and ensure a consistent framework across all courts dealing with family matters so that, for example, it is easier to transfer cases between courts. Application forms are standard for all courts. The FPC rules refer to 'family proceedings' and 'specified proceedings'.

'Family proceedings'
When a case falls within this definition (see *Part Two* of this handbook), then—irrespective of the subject matter of the application—the court can *of its own motion* make any section 8 order (*Chapter 2*) in respect of any child concerned. Thus, for example, if a local authority applies for a care order (a matter within the definition), the court can make a residence order instead, or a contact order as well, if this is in the best interests of the child. Lawyers in *private law* cases should forewarn their clients of the court's wide-ranging powers. For example, if a mother and father disagree over where a child should live and one applies for a residence order, it is open to the court to consider whether an order should be made in favour of someone else like a grandparent who would provide the child with a better home and upbringing.

'Specified proceedings'
The full definition of 'specified proceedings' is contained in *Part Two* of this handbook. The main points to note when a case falls within the definition are that:

- the child is a *party* to the proceedings
- the child will not normally appear in court, but an independent guardian ad litem (*Chapter 4*) will invariably be appointed to safeguard the child's interests, submit a report and attend in the child's place; and
- the guardian will instruct a solicitor to act for the child.

Most specified proceedings occur in *public law* cases—notably care proceedings (*Chapter 2*).

MAKING AN APPLICATION: KEY POINTS

Applications are started by filing a 'core' form (C1). Particularly vis-à-vis *public law* cases—a 'supplement' is required. A schedule of forms and supplements appears at the end of the FPC rules. No other documents can be used. This contrasts with the situation in criminal cases where magistrates' courts may adapt forms to suit local or other circumstances. Often, a great deal of information has to be supplied. Thus, for example, Form C1 (with supplement C13 used in care proceedings)—both of which are reproduced in *Part Two* of this handbook—asks for details of:

- the child and his or her family
- current, past or pending proceedings in respect of the child
- existing parental responsibility
- reasons for believing that the 'threshold criteria' are met
- the local authority's plans for the child and its views about who should be allowed contact with the child.

If an applicant cannot give complete answers this will usually be accepted by the court, particularly if the matter is urgent, but he or she will be expected to make reasonable efforts to obtain missing information and provide this as soon as practicable. If the facts alter, the party concerned must inform the court. Other points to note include:

- the applicant need only fill in *one* application form per family, even if more than one application is made
- fees are payable. In May 1997, the fee is £30 for each *private law* application and £50 for every *public law* application. Fees are not payable if the applicant is legally aided, on income based job seekers allowance or in receipt of family credit, evidence of which must be provided. The court or justices' clerk can remit fees if this is thought to be in the applicant's interest

- the applicant must provide sufficient copies for the court and respondents (below). Where applicants do not have a lawyer, court staff normally assist (and may produce copies without charge)
- the court allocates a unique reference number to *each child* mentioned in the application. It then attaches a 'notice of proceedings' for each respondent, containing guidance notes and the date and time when the first directions appointment or hearing will take place. This date will allow time for the applicant to serve the forms—and give respondents the statutory period of notice (e.g. for a section 8 application, 14 days). Schedule 2 to the FPC rules gives the notice periods for various kinds of application. The court can give leave for shorter notice if appropriate
- the applicant is responsible for serving copies on the respondents. The court does not undertake this role.

Ex parte applications

There are various situations in which an application for an order can be made *ex parte*, the most common being in relation to emergency protection orders (*Chapter 2*) and pressing section 8 matters (*Chapter 2*). *Ex parte* applications require leave and, as always, sound reasons must exist before this will be given. Magistrates cannot grant this variety of leave, only the justices' clerk or a duly authorised legal advisor. All courts should operate a 24 hour call out system, and can deal with such applications over the telephone.

There may frequently be *urgency* in having an application heard, but this is not the same thing as saying that there is an *immediate need* for an order—and that this justifies dispensing with notice to the parties or their attendance. If leave *is* given, the court will make arrangements for the application to be heard without delay and give directions. If a prohibited steps order, specific issue order or emergency protection order is granted in this way, the applicant must serve a copy of the application and the order within 48 hours of its being made.

Ex parte applications rare in section 8 cases

Whereas a large number of emergency protection orders are still made *ex parte*, the occasions when it is appropriate to grant a section 8 order in this way are rare. In *Re G (Minors) (Ex parte residence order)* (1992) 2 FCR 720 the Court of Appeal said that it should be very rare indeed for there to be an *ex parte* residence order, although such an approach might be appropriate in a 'snatch situation' (e.g. where one party is about to make off with a child, possibly heading abroad) or to protect a child in other exceptional circumstances. In *Y v B, The Independent*, 15 February 1993 it was stated that it is highly undesirable for *ex parte* orders to stand for more than seven days (although they can legally do so where the situation is exceptional).

Withdrawing an application

An application under the 1989 Act can only be withdrawn with the leave of the court. A form must be completed and served on the court and all other parties. Cogent reasons are needed. Case law indicates that such a request must be listened to as carefully as an application for an order. The requirement of a written request is dispensed with if the proceedings are before the court and all parties are present, together with any guardian ad litem or welfare officer. The classic instance occurs following mediation, when agreement is reached and the court is satisfied that the proposals are in the best interests of the child.

Bar to further applications

The family proceedings court can make an order requiring someone to obtain leave before making a further application: seek legal advice.

THE PARTIES

Parties are known as *applicants* and *respondents*. Normally, any interested person can apply for an order in respect of a child, but only a local authority (in practice through its social services department) or the NSPCC can apply for a care or supervision order. With section 8 orders, the law recognises two kinds of people:

- those with an *absolute right* to apply (e.g. a parent); and
- those who need leave (e.g. grandparents, a stranger).

Applications for leave can be heard *ex parte*, or the court can order a special preliminary hearing involving the applicant and potential respondents. Full reasons should support any application. Certain principles must be observed:

- a *Practice Direction* (1993) 1 ALL ER 82 indicates that applications *by children* for leave to apply for a section 8 order must be heard in the High Court, when that court will consider whether the child is mature enough to understand the consequences
- in respect of most applications for leave to apply for a section 8 order the court must consider criteria laid down by the 1989 Act:

— the nature of the application
— the applicant's connection with the child
— the risk of harmful disruption to the child
— where the child is being 'looked after' by the local authority, that authority's plans for the child and the wishes and feelings of the child's parents.

When assessing whether a child is 'at risk of disruption' a court can consider the potential outcome, i.e. if the substantive application succeeds—for example the impact if the applicant became involved in the child's life. The court is also entitled to consider other relevant matters, including the child's wishes.

The Court of Appeal upheld a decision by family panel magistrates who—when dealing with an application for leave—set up a preliminary hearing, permitted extensive cross-examination on matters going to the merits of the proposed main application, and sought the views of all concerned. The court must apply basic principles of justice. Thus, in another case, magistrates were held wrong to refuse leave—without hearing oral evidence from the main parties—to a grandmother who wished to apply for a contact order. Had it done so, the court could have formed a view as to disputed facts, the merits of the application and any risk of harm to the children. However, the fact that someone obtains leave does *not* imply any presumption in favour of that party at the final hearing.

Respondents
It is important for the applicant and the court to know who the respondents are. The applicant must serve all respondents with a copy of the application (and any supplement)—and, generally speaking, they have a right to attend hearings and to give evidence. Schedule 2 to the FPC Rules lists the people who have an *automatic right* to be made a respondent as well as people who should be notified but who are not parties as a matter of course. A common example of the latter is a foster parent who has been looking after a child under a care order which the court is being asked to discharge. People can become respondents in various ways:

- by applying to the court in writing (sometimes called 'asking for leave to intervene')
- the court may direct that someone who would not otherwise be a respondent should be joined as a party
- the guardian ad litem has a statutory duty to notify the court if he or she thinks people ought to be parties (the main basis upon

which the court adds respondents in practice). Welfare officers are not under the same duty, but often alert courts to people it may wish to consider adding.

The President of the Family Division has expressed concern about the number of parties in some *public law* cases. A survey showed that in the early years of the 1989 Act, 51 per cent of cases involved at least five parties—and the worst instance eleven. The Court of Appeal criticised a case where grandparents were given leave to intervene where their interests were identical with those of the parents. The judges commented that, particularly in *private law* cases, relatives should not seek to become parties unless they have a separate point of view. In one case, it was held that someone seeking leave to intervene must establish that his or her application is reasonably likely to succeed. The High Court had refused to allow an aunt to be joined as a party when there was no reasonable prospect of her obtaining a residence or contact order. In another *public law* case parents each had a separate lawyer although not in conflict. This was unnecessary duplication and a waste of time and cost—the 'enemies of justice'!

The modern practice is for legal representatives aware of people who support their client's case to ask the court for leave to treat them *as witnesses*—rather than for them to become respondents.

SERVICE OF DOCUMENTS

Documents can be served:

- if the other party has a solicitor, by delivering them personally to the solicitor's office or sending them there by first class post, and also by document exchange or facsimile
- if the other party is not so represented, then only by delivering them personally or sending them by first class post
- as directed by the court or justices' clerk in an individual case.

Acknowledgement by the respondent

When dealing with any section 8 application, the court must attach an acknowledgement of service to be given to the respondent. This must be completed by each respondent and served on the court and other parties within 14 days of its receipt. It also requires the respondent to indicate whether he or she is going to oppose the application or apply for any other order. Respondents are often not represented by a lawyer—and may not comply with these instructions. Although the court can make them pay costs in such a situation, in practice, rightly or wrongly, courts are often 'tolerant'. By being otherwise, justice may ultimately be defeated.

DIRECTIONS

Case management takes place against the background of 'allocation' and 'directions'.

Allocation

As described in *Chapter 1*, most family proceedings start in the magistrates' court and are then allocated to one of three tiers of court which share this jurisdiction—the High Court, county court or magistrates' family proceedings court. Allocation is by the justices' clerk (or an authorised legal advisor). It is open to the parties to seek a review by the magistrates of the allocation decision, or to ask at a court hearing for the case to be transferred elsewhere.

Directions appointments

If a case *is* allocated to the family proceedings court, the next step is to decide what directions (in essence 'instructions') should be given to the applicant and, in due course, other parties to the case. Directions seek to avoid cases reaching court—or at least until they are ready to proceed— and to enhance the way they are dealt with when they do reach court. Directions can be given *at any time* (and can be varied or revoked):

- by the court *of its own motion* after notice of its intention to do so, and an opportunity for the party or parties to make oral or written representations
- at the *written request of a party* specifying the direction sought, either:
  —a 'one party' application, which must be filed with the court and served on the other parties before it can be considered, for example where one party believes that a child should be medically examined
  —by consent, when the application must be countersigned, or otherwise accepted in writing, by the other party or parties (usually via legal representatives). The court still has a discretion whether to make the direction, but straightforward cases are frequently dealt with 'in absence'.

If attendance *is* required, the court must normally give at least two days notice. In urgent cases, a request for a direction can be made orally and without notice to other parties (i.e. *ex parte*). The leave of the court—and a valid reason—is needed before such an application can proceed.

Who gives directions?
Directions can be given by:

- the court
- any member of the family panel
- the justices' clerk (or an authorised legal advisor).

During the *preliminary stages*, the practice in many areas of the country is for the justices' clerk to deal with such matters. Where the need for directions occurs *in the course of a full or interim court hearing*, the court itself can give the direction—subject to any appropriate legal advice.

The justices' clerk (or legal advisor) has virtually all the powers of a single magistrate to give directions, but he or she cannot make someone a respondent (above).

Parties and their legal representatives must attend directions appointments unless given leave not to do so. Actual practice varies. Some courts require both to be present so that immediate instructions can be taken if the court is considering a particular course. Others are content for only the lawyers to be there. Some courts will also accept attendance by a suitably qualified legal executive (seek advice locally). There may be a change in the law to sanction this practice.

The guardian ad litem is deemed to be a party and should attend. A welfare officer must do so if specifically required to.

What directions appointments seek to achieve
The FPC rules give a list of directions, but this is not exhaustive. Case law emphasises the need for courts to be proactive. In practice, directions appointments seek to deal with such items as:

- *what is in dispute*
- *whether there is a chance of agreement* including whether the case should be referred for mediation
- *who the parties are* and whether any should be added (above)
- *appointment of a guardian ad litem or welfare officer* This is often done when the application is received. If not, it can be dealt with at the first appointment, reports can be requested and a timescale for these set

- *whether expert evidence is involved* and later whether experts have conferred with each other (below)
- *how long the final hearing will take* including the times at which witnesses should be called. Where the case *does* proceed to a full hearing, directions can be given requiring the preparation of a 'bundle' of documents including a chronology showing the major events in the child's life so that the magistrates dealing with the case have the full picture, rather than having to piece this together from disparate application forms, statements and reports
- *a timetable* to stop 'drift' and undue delay. At the earliest opportunity, time limits will be laid down within which certain acts must be done. In many areas, objectives and targets have been agreed through inter-agency collaboration
- *varying time limits* There is a discretion to alter the notice periods in the FPC rules, but *not retrospectively*
- *attendance by the child* For some children this can be a harmful experience, whilst in other cases the child wants to be at court. Guidance from the guardian ad litem or welfare officer may be crucial. Case law makes clear that it should only be in exceptional circumstances that a child actually attends court. The Magistrates' Association has for some time felt that in appropriate cases it may be in the interests of a child for him or her to be present, particularly in the relatively informal atmosphere of the family proceedings court. However, in 1996, Sir Stephen Brown, President of the Family Division, speaking extra-judicially, reiterated that case law stating that children should not normally be in court applies equally to family proceedings courts
- *service of documents* where the normal rules (above) cannot be complied with or it is desirable for them to be departed from
- *submission of evidence* (including expert reports). The 'standard direction' suggested by the Children Act Advisory Committee suggests that the statement of a party should *not* be filed until after sight of any welfare report—and should then be limited to the findings in that report with which he or she disagrees, or relevant matters not covered by it. This interventionist approach can considerably restrict what a party can say—but it is not being adopted in practice by all family proceedings courts
- *whether there should be a 'split hearing'* Findings of fact (e.g. sexual abuse or non-accidental injury) must occur before questions of welfare can be addressed. In an appropriate case consideration can be given whether a direction should be made that the 'threshold criteria' be addressed promptly—in advance of other features of the case—by way of a 'split hearing'.

Courts have developed 'standard directions'—although their application varies from one place to another. Copies may be available locally on request. The Children Act Advisory Committee has published sample directions as a starting point for courts. A selection of specimen directions is contained in *Part Two* of this handbook.

Practice Direction (Family proceedings: Case management) (1995) 1 FLR 456 issued by the President of the Family Division deals with judicial concern about delay. The direction indicates that failing to conduct cases economically can incur orders for costs, including 'wasted costs' (see *Costs*, below and the further explanation in *Materials F, Item 8*). The direction also states that courts can limit:

- discovery (i.e. the extent to which parties can obtain information about the other party's case). Conversely, there is a duty to make full and frank disclosure. There is a similar duty for a party to use his or her best endeavours to confine issues and evidence to what is essential, and to agree in advance the main issues outstanding
- opening and closing speeches
- cross-examination
- reading from documents, etc.

It is open via directions to specify, for example, that:

- an opening speech will not be longer than 'X minutes'
- every witness statement can stand as the evidence-in-chief of the witness. When a witness takes the oath and identifies his or her statement it is then treated as that witness' evidence, subject to any supplementary questions to clarify matters and cross-examination by other parties. Similarly, witness statements must be confined to material matters of fact, and be sufficiently detailed but not prolix.
- 'bundles' (i.e. of documents) should be agreed in advance.

The *Practice Direction* applies only to the county court and High Court, but in a letter to the Justices' Clerks' Society the President indicated that the same principles apply to the family proceedings court. The above outline has been adapted accordingly.

Amendment
No document or form can be amended without the leave of the court. The request for leave must be in writing unless the court directs otherwise. The court can either grant the request to amend 'in absence'

or can invite representations. Relevant documents must be filed or served in the usual way.

SEEING A CHILD 'IN PRIVATE'

The Court of Appeal has given guidance concerning seeing a child in private, for example in the magistrates' retiring room:

> The court does indeed have a discretion to see children privately in any case which relates to their upbringing, but it is a discretion which should be exercised cautiously.

The guidance emphasises that there must be a good reason to see the child—and the court must be satisfied that it is in his or her interests to do so *in private*. The court should first hear submissions from the parties, and make clear that what is said in private cannot be withheld from the parents. Whilst there is a discretion as to *when* to see a child, the normal time is after the evidence of witnesses and before any closing speeches. The views of the child are important, but the final decision is for the court.

THE HEARING

Court hearings involve a degree of informality, albeit that they are thoughtfully structured to encourage full and frank exchanges concerning the best interests of the child. Some of the main points to note about the arrangements in the family proceedings court (which mirror those in the county court and High Court) are that:

- the magistrates must read all documents before going into court. This includes the application form, witness statements and reports
- the court decides what evidence it wishes to hear and in what order. A justices' clerk, court legal advisor or magistrate at a directions appointment, or the court or advisor at the hearing, may give directions as to the order of speeches and evidence.

If the court does not give specific directions, the evidence will usually proceed, for example in a *public law* case, as follows:

- the applicant
- any party with parental responsibility

- other respondents
- the guardian ad litem
- the child if he or she is a party (and, unusually, no guardian ad litem has been appointed).

Interim hearings

It was once common practice for hearings held at an interim stage to be used as a 'dress rehearsal' for the main hearing—and for this to occupy an inordinate length of time. Modern guidelines (which apply, with appropriate adaptation, to both *public law* and *private law* cases) are:

- an interim order (or short term order) is only a 'holding order' until the substantive hearing—but nevertheless courts must consider any relevant risks pending that hearing and ensure that the substantive issue is heard at the earliest possible time
- courts should rarely make findings on disputed facts at the interim stage. These should be left to the final hearing
- courts should be cautious about changing a child's residence. The preferred course is to leave the child in the same place—with safeguards—and set an early hearing date
- if an interim order would lead to a substantial change in the child's position the court should hear limited oral evidence. Evidence and cross-examination should be restricted to issues essential to the interim stage
- the court should intervene to prevent a 'dress rehearsal'
- the court should ensure that it has written advice from the guardian ad litem (or welfare officer). A party opposed to any advice should be given the opportunity to put questions
- on granting interim relief, magistrates should state their findings and reasons concisely and summarise briefly the essential factual issues between the parties—although they will not be able to make findings on disputed facts as the court will not have heard all the evidence.

Some points about the evidence

In *civil cases* the burden of proof rests with the person making a particular assertion, usually the applicant, to prove matters to the required standard of proof, i.e. on a balance of probabilities. In *Re H and R (Child Sexual Abuse: Standard of Proof)* (1996) 1 FLR 80, the House of Lords decided that a local authority bringing care proceedings on the basis of significant harm in the future must prove that there is a real possibility of risk based on *facts* rather than *suspicions*. It was also stated that there are not different standards of proof depending on the type of allegation. However, the more serious the allegation, the 'more convincing' was the evidence needed to tip the balance in respect of it.

Oral evidence

Normally, oral evidence will only be capable of being given at a court hearing if, in advance, a written statement setting out its substance:

- is served on the parties and the court in accordance with directions; or
- in the absence of any such direction, before the hearing.

A statement must be dated and signed, and contain a declaration that the maker believes the contents to be true and understands that it may be placed before the court. This also applies to any report. If the requirements are not complied with, the leave of the court must be obtained before the associated oral evidence can be given. There must be a good reason why the disclosure requirements were not complied with. The court can refuse to admit evidence which has not been filed in accordance with a direction.

Even more stringent requirements apply to section 8 cases. The FPC rules require that a party shall:

- not file nor serve any document other than those required or authorised by the rules
- in completing a form prescribed by the rules, not give information or make a statement unless required or authorised by that form without leave; and that
- no statement or copy may be filed until such time as the justices' clerk, a magistrate or the court directs.

These 'sub-rules' are designed to give the court a high level of control of the proceedings and ensure that documents concentrate on the welfare of the child. The applicant and respondent are restricted to answering questions in the forms and cannot introduce other items or evidence without leave. No statement can be filed until the court decides it is appropriate to do this. This allows for the possibility of reconciliation or conciliation before damaging statements are made. Practitioners need to be alert to these rules and sensitive to their underlying aims.

Self incrimination

Particularly in care proceedings prior to the Children Act 1989, a difficulty occurred if a parent or other party was being prosecuted for criminal offences directly connected with the facts behind the care proceedings. Thus, for example, if the (then) ground for the care proceedings was ill-treatment and the father or mother was being prosecuted for a related assault, if the parent gave evidence in the care proceedings this evidence might be used against him or her in the criminal prosecution. If he or she did not give evidence, then the court dealing with the care proceedings was deprived of highly relevant information.

The 1989 Act—in encouraging all relevant evidence to surface—effects a compromise. Section 98 provides that in any proceedings in which a court is hearing an application for an order under Part IV or V of the Act, nobody shall be excused from:

- giving evidence on any matter; or
- answering any question put to him or her in the course of giving evidence

on the ground that doing so might incriminate him or her, or his or her spouse. However, an admission made in such proceedings is not admissible in evidence against the person making it—or his or her spouse—in proceedings for an offence other than perjury. In the example above, the parent could give evidence in care proceedings and would have to answer any relevant questions. However, any evidence given could not be used in a forthcoming trial for assault. In *Re G* (1996) 1 FLR 276 it was held that section 98 does not come into play unless and until objection is taken to the admission of evidence in a criminal trial.

The above rules only apply to *public law* cases. Thus, for example, they do *not* apply to an application for a 'section 8' order where the traditional rules against self-incrimination continue in effect.

Hearsay

Generally speaking in a court of law, evidence must be 'first-hand', an account which is within the knowledge of the witness—i.e. *not* hearsay. The Children (Admissibility of Hearsay Evidence) Order 1991 brought into force from 14 October 1991 vis-à-vis family proceedings courts, various provisions affecting evidence about the upbringing, maintenance and welfare of a child. In effect, such evidence became admissible notwithstanding the rule against hearsay. Thus, for example, a social worker is able to give evidence based on notes made by a colleague, possibly no longer in post. The order renders such evidence *admissible*. It leaves the decision about what *weight* should be attached to it to the court. Thus, if first hand evidence *is* available, it remains preferable to use it.

51

Also, at the time of writing (May, 1997), the Civil Evidence Act 1995 awaits rules affecting its implementation. Subject to safeguards, the 1995 Act will permit hearsay evidence in *all* civil proceedings. It is understood, however, that the Act will *not* be applied to Children Act cases and that the 'hearsay order' outlined above will continue to apply to this type of case.

FINDINGS OF FACT AND REASONS

The justices' clerk or court legal advisor must record in writing the names of the magistrates and—in consultation with them:

- their findings of fact; and
- the reasons for their decision.

As a result of these requirements—and subject to any reserved decision (below)—a party wishing to appeal can obtain the court's reasons immediately and in writing. The obligation applies to *all* applications under the 1989 Act, whether for a final order, interim order or other intermediate decision. Since reasons have to be put into writing *at the time of the hearing,* magistrates will require time to undertake this aspect. As indicated in *Chapter 1,* good practice indicates that the legal advisor needs to be with the magistrates throughout their discussions. Outline structures for the process of fact finding and reason giving are contained in *Part Two* of this handbook.

Reserved decisions
The court must reach a decision *as soon as practicable.* However, it need not do this immediately the evidence and speeches finish. It may well be wrong to rush into a decision after hearing evidence all day. It can reserve judgment, when ideally it should reconvene the following day to make and announce its decision—and give its reasons

DUTIES OF LEGAL REPRESENTATIVES

In *B v B (Court Bundles Video Evidence)* 1994 1 FLR 323 guidance was given on how to prepare for a trial. This is summarised in *Part Two* of this handbook as an indication of the standards magistrates can expect from legal representatives. Practitioners are also referred to the Justices' Clerks' Society *Good Practice Guide for Listing Family Cases* (1996) which has been approved by the Children Act Advisory Committee and the President of the Family Division.

EXPERTS

Whereas ordinary witnesses are confined to matters of *fact*, experts can give evidence of their *opinions* where these fall within the scope of their expertise. It is for the court to decide who to accept as an expert—on the basis of the witness' professional or other qualifications and experience. Medical practitioners, psychiatrists and similar professionals regularly give evidence or provide reports to courts in family matters. There is a great deal of guidance to courts on the topic and particularly concerning the sort of directions that should be given. The Children Act Advisory Committee's fourth annual report stated:

> The case of *Re AB (A Minor) (Child Abuse: Expert Witnesses)* (1995) 1 FLR 181 is a reminder that it is of critical importance to note the respective functions of expert and judge. The expert forms an assessment and expresses an opinion within the area of his expertise. The judge decides particular issues in individual cases. It is not for the judge to become involved in medical controversy, except in the rare case where such controversy is an issue in the case. The court depends on the skill, knowledge and above all the professional and intellectual integrity of the expert witness.

Where experts are instructed:

- general orders for leave to disclose case papers to an expert should never be made. On the contrary, the area of expertise, the issues to be addressed and the particular expert should be identified in advance of appointment, thereby facilitating a timetable for the preparation and submission of the report, and the availability of the expert to give evidence if required
- advocates who seek leave to instruct experts must place *all* relevant information before the court at the earliest opportunity. The court has a duty to enquire into that information, and in particular:
  —the category of expert evidence, the name of the expert and his or her availability
  —the relevance to the issues
  —whether the evidence can properly be obtained by *joint instruction* of one expert by all parties
  —whether expert evidence may properly be adduced by one party only, for example the guardian ad litem
- applications to instruct experts should be considered at the earliest possible stage to avoid 'serial applications' later on by parties seeking to counter unsupportive opinions

- reports based solely upon a 'paper exercise' are rarely as persuasive as those based on interviews, personal assessment and full documentation
- *Re C (Expert Evidence: Disclosure Practice)* (1995) 1 FLR 204 provides guidance about experts in contested cases conferring in advance of the hearing. It should be a condition of their appointment that they do so and identify areas of agreement or dispute. These should be set out—in good time—in a schedule for the court and parties. Ideally, the court should ask the guardian ad litem (or welfare officer) to coordinate this.

Among other cases, those of *Re M (Minors) (Care Proceedings: Child's Wishes)* (1994) 1 FLR 749 and *Re T and E (Proceedings: Conflicting Interests)* (1995) 1 FLR 581 give further guidance concerning the mechanics of obtaining expert evidence and other information about the duties of experts: see *Part Two* of this handbook.

COSTS

Appeal rulings make it clear that costs should only be awarded in family cases in exceptional circumstances. Nonetheless, the court has wide powers—at any time in the proceedings—to make an order that one party pay the whole or any part of the costs of any other party. The party against whom a court is considering awarding costs must be given an opportunity to make representations.

The Courts and Legal Services Act 1990 sets out the circumstances in which, effectively, a solicitor may be personally liable for costs, i.e. if the court feels that he or she was primarily to blame for any delay, omission, etc: seek legal advice. See also *Practice Direction (Family proceedings: Case management)* (1995) under the heading *Directions*, above.

Although directions hearings do not form part of the family proceedings courts' decision—and therefore costs may *not* be allowed or disallowed—it is likely that a subsequent formal family proceedings court hearing connected to those proceedings does have the power to make an order of wasted costs in relation to a previous direction.

APPEAL

There is a general right of appeal to the High Court against the making or refusal to make most orders under the 1989 Act. The procedure is set out in a *Practice Direction* of 31 January 1992. Case law establishes that appellants must ensure that all documents (in typescript) are lodged with the District Registry of the High Court and that the court is alerted to any urgency.

Magistrates cannot 'stay' (i.e. sus pend) a care order pending appeal. If this is required, the proper course is to apply to the High Court immediately.

On appeal the High Court has wide ranging powers to deal with the case in any way in which the family proceedings court could have dealt with it, but is not empowered to hear evidence except in exceptional circumstances.

Appeals are governed by principles stated by the House of Lords in *G v G* 1985 1 WLR 647. In essence, where the decision involves an exercise of discretion—i.e. the magistrates preferring one view of the facts to another, or one particular view of the child's best interests—the appeal court will not interfere unless it considers that they were plainly wrong, erred in principle, took into account something that they should not have done, or failed to take into account something that they should have done. Courts can only act on relevant considerations—and must not ignore any relevant matters.

CHAPTER 4

Welfare of the Child

Ever since the Children and Young Persons Act 1933, *all* courts dealing with children must have regard to their welfare. Section 1 Children Act 1989 stipulates that:

- the child's welfare is the paramount consideration
- the court should not make an order unless it considers that to do so would be better for the child than making no order at all; and
- the court should have regard to the general principle that delay in determining a question with respect to the upbringing of a child is likely to prejudice the welfare of the child.

Welfare the paramount consideration

All three limbs of section 1 concern welfare, the first stipulation being all-embracing and the subject matter of the rest of this chapter which deals with the principles involved and the methods by which these are delivered in practice.

The presumption of no order

If in a *public law case* a local authority is trying to persuade the court to make a care order, not only does it have to establish one of the threshold criteria outlined in *Chapter 2* but it must go on to convince the court that making a care or supervision order would be better than making no order at all. The court will need to be satisfied about the local authority's plans for the child, that these are in the child's best interests and can only be achieved via a court order.

It is the same in *private law* cases when the court is deciding whether to make a section 8 order for, say, contact with a relative (and even when deciding whether to grant leave to apply for an order in those circumstances where it must also consider the likelihood of an order being made: *Chapter 3*). It may be that agreement can be reached instead, or encouraged through mediation.

Avoiding delay

One criticism of the pre-1989 law was that contested cases took too long and, for children especially—who because of the relative shortness of their lives experience weeks, months and years in a different 'time-frame' to adults—prolonged periods of uncertainty could be damaging. The principle that delay should be avoided never rules out proper enquiries, for example, to see whether there is a possibility of agreement between the parties without recourse to a full court hearing, or an adjournment where some positive action is taking place (such as a medical or psychiatric assessment). It is meant to stop *drift*, i.e. delay which is not justified. The principle is reinforced by:

- the system of allocations and directions (*Chapters 1* and *3*)
- the requirement for the court to draw up a timetable (*Chapter 3*); and
- a number of Best Practice guides and National Standards affecting courts or agencies serving the family proceedings court.

Remarkably, delay *increased* following the Children Act 1989 and Dame Margaret Booth (a former High Court judge) was commissioned by the Lord Chancellor to research the causes of this. Her report *Avoiding Delay in Children Act Cases* (1996) indicates that systems operating in family cases are basically sound, but courts and justices' clerks need to be pro-active in seeking to avoid delay, particularly when giving directions and in relation to case management generally: *Chapter 3*.

POST-1989 EMPHASIS

As discussed in earlier chapters, the emphasis in family work is on avoiding conflict, encouraging agreement and not intervening unless in the child's best interests. *Whenever* a case is before the family proceedings court, there is a free-standing duty to consider the welfare of any children and, if appropriate, to use the court's powers to safeguard that welfare. This is reinforced by provisions under which:

- in *private law* cases (i.e. applications by individuals such as parents or grandparents) the court can ask for a welfare report. The preparation of such reports is the responsibility of the Family Court Welfare Service (which operates under the auspices of the Probation Service). It can also direct investigations by a local authority (*Chapter 2*)
- in *public law* cases (i.e. applications by local authorities) the court can, and usually will, appoint a guardian ad litem from a panel of independent guardians. He or she will represent the child, report to the court and appoint a solicitor from the Law Society Children Panel to act for the child.

The role of the Court Welfare Service and that of the independent guardian ad litem are dealt with later in this chapter.

The philosophy of welfare

Other important messages can be gleaned from the 1989 Act, legal rulings, reports and discussion papers as follows:

- wherever possible, children should be brought up and cared for within their own families and by both parents
- parents with children 'in need' (including disabled children) should be helped to bring up their children themselves.

The support offered to a child and his or her family should:

- be provided *in partnership* with his or her parents
- meet the child's identifiable needs
- be appropriate in terms of the child's race, culture, religion and linguistic background
- draw on effective collaboration between the various agencies, including those in the voluntary sector
- ensure that children are safe, and protected by intervention if in danger (albeit that intervention must be open to challenge)
- provide adequate standards of care and high-quality substitute parenting if a child has no parents, or when parents cannot offer this themselves
- involve consulting and listening to the child and keeping him or her informed about what is happening to them
- safeguard contact with parents and the child's wider family who have a role in their children's lives, even when they live apart from them.

In the case of local authorities, these considerations are reinforced by independent representations and complaints procedures. Also, situations where children are cared for outside of their own family or live away from home are open to scrutiny and review, to ensure that adequate standards of care and safety are maintained and that children are not kept away from their families where the situation does not continue to merit this. Courts must ensure that their decisions take account of the above items as appropriate, that they are responsive to the needs of children and that any orders are designed to promote the child's welfare.

THE WELFARE CHECKLIST

The 1989 Act provides a 'checklist'. In most *public law* and contested *private law* cases, section 1(3) states that the court must have regard, in particular, to:

(a) the ascertainable wishes and feelings of the child concerned (considered in the light of his age and understanding);

(b) his physical, emotional and educational needs;

(c) the likely effect on him of any change in his circumstances;

(d) his age, sex, background and any characteristics of his which the court considers relevant;

(e) any harm which he has suffered or is at risk of suffering;

(f) how capable each of his parents, and any other person in relation to whom the court considers the question to be relevant, is of meeting his needs;

(g) the range of powers available to the court under this Act in the proceedings in question.

As a matter of practice, the checklist is used in *all* Children Act cases. The items build on former case law, but two were new:

- a direct reference to *the wishes and feelings of the child;* and
- mention of the *range of powers* available to the court.

The idea that children should be consulted about decisions affecting them was already established good practice and its inclusion in statute reflects the fact that too little emphasis may have been placed on listening to children in the past. However, the fact that the child's wishes and general feelings must be considered does not mean that they are the determining factor, or that the child should be made 'to choose'. Good practice in dealing with children involves taking their views and preferences into account. This can only be achieved if there is effective communication between the child and other people in the case, including welfare officers, guardians ad litem and legal representatives. There is a similar need for such people to prepare a child for appearing in court when this is necessary and unavoidable.

The fact that the welfare checklist includes 'the range of powers available to the court' reflects how the 1989 Act altered and increased the court's decision-making options. As outlined in *Chapter 2*, it can make certain orders of its own motion in *any* family proceedings.

THE FAMILY COURT WELFARE SERVICE

The Family Court Welfare Service operates under the auspices of the Probation Service. The principle tasks of the court welfare officer (CWO) are, at the request of the court:

- to meet the parties before or during a directions appointment for preliminary assessment and to identify areas of agreement

- to meet the parties at the direction of the court to assist them to make agreed decisions about their children
- to carry out enquiries and prepare a welfare report to assist the court.

The Home Office, in consultation with the Lord Chancellor's Department, the Department of Health and the Welsh Office, has issued National Standards for Probation Service Family Court Welfare Work which are designed to ensure consistency, fairness and good practice and that everyone dealing with CWOs is clear what to expect. The standards state that:

> the primary objective of all family court welfare work undertaken by the probation service is to help the courts in their task of serving the needs of children whose parents are involved in disputes in private law.

The standards refer to the main principles of the 1989 Act and state that these underpin the work involved.

The court welfare officer
The CWO is someone who, after general training and practice as a probation officer, specialises in family work. Selection interviews are held and once appointed CWOs undergo training to equip them for this specialism. Many CWOs stay in family work for the rest of their careers (although a five year period in the role is recommended). Probation areas have agreed jointly negotiated 'written agreements' or 'protocols' with local courts, a process often undertaken in consultation with the local Family Court Business Committee. The main tasks in which the Family Court Welfare Service are likely to be involved include:

Early assistance
This involves meeting the parties to a private law case (e.g. concerning contact with, or the residence of, a child) at an early stage to make a preliminary assessment and identify:

- any areas of agreement
- what issues, if any, are in dispute; and
- whether there is any chance of agreement being reached without the continued involvement of the court.

Courts usually list section 8 cases for an early directions appointment. The CWO can then assist the court or justices' clerk from the outset to decide upon the best way of managing the case. The CWO's discussions with the parties at this stage are normally brief (and are *not privileged*). It is important that the parties are aware of the reasons for the meeting and consent to it. Any objections by a party, for example because of allegations of violence or abuse, should be drawn to the attention of the court.

Following the initial meeting, the CWO and the parties can report to the court on progress. If agreement *has* been reached—and subject to any legal advice which the parties may require before considering whether to go along with that agreement—then:

- if no order is necessary the applicant can ask to withdraw the application
- if an order does seem to be necessary the court can consider whether to proceed to a final consent order; or
- the case can be adjourned for a suitable period to test the agreement, with or without recourse to an order.

However, if at this initial stage it is *not* possible to resolve matters, the CWO, together with the parties and their legal representatives, will present the situation to the court. The court's options then include:

- referring the case for mediation (below). It will then be adjourned for such action and progress will be reported to the court at the next hearing; or
- calling for a welfare report on matters in dispute, which the court will specify.

Mediation

Mediation, sometimes called 'conciliation', is a process involving the parties in *privileged* discussions with a third party (the mediator) in an attempt to resolve disputes, in the present context, over the welfare of children. Mediation discussions *are* privileged (contrast the CWO's initial discussions with the parties, above) which means that anything said may only be reported to the court if all parties to the proceedings involved in the discussions agree. There is an exception where, during mediation, something is said which indicates a risk of serious harm to the child.

It is important that the parties understand what this process involves and give informed consent. Normally, mediation takes place away from the court premises and may be conducted by the court welfare officer or a trained independent mediator. According to National Standards, the aims are:

- to facilitate communications between the parties in dispute
- to identify and clarify the issues about which there is conflict; and

- to remind parties of their continuing parental responsibility for their children and that their welfare is paramount; and
- to encourage and help parties to reach an agreement which is in the best interests of the child.

If agreement is reached, the CWO should provide each party with a copy to discuss with their legal representative (if any). At the court hearing following mediation, the parties and their lawyers ask for:

- leave to withdraw the application based on the fact that no order is now necessary
- a final consent order based on the agreement; or
- an adjournment to test the agreement, again with or without an interim or short term order (*Chapter 2*) as appropriate.

As with all agreed orders, the court itself must be satisfied that the agreement is in the best interests of the child and that it is right to endorse it. If no agreement is reached this fact is reported at the next court hearing. It is then likely that the court will request a welfare report. If the CWO *has* undertaken the mediation, another officer must be assigned to the case and should not be given access to any statements made or information given during the mediation.

Welfare Reports

Section 7 Children Act 1989 provides that when the court is considering 'any question with respect to a child' under the 1989 Act, the court may ask a probation officer (i.e. usually the CWO) or an officer of the local authority (a social worker) to report to the court on any matters relating to the welfare of that child. The purpose of a welfare report is to provide the court with information which will enable it to make decisions which are in the best interests of the child. Normally the report is in writing except in situations where there is a verbal addendum or information is urgent.

Courts often have local agreements setting out which agency should respond to the request for a welfare report, but as a general rule the CWO deals with the majority of such requests in *private law* disputes unless there is some special reason to request otherwise.

Although the report writer should help the parties to reach agreement if he or she sees an opportunity for this during his or her enquiries, it is not the role of the CWO to set out to resolve disputes when preparing a report. Rather, the purpose is to enquire professionally and impartially.

The CWO will require a period in which to complete his or her enquiries and a date by which he or she should file the report with the court is given as a direction. Periods vary around the country (and with the nature of the case) from eight weeks up to 26 weeks. However, National Standards indicate that the report should be filed within ten weeks of receipt of the papers by the Family Court Welfare Service.

To ensure that the nature and scope of the enquiries match the circumstances of the case and reflect matters which the court wants to see dealt with, courts have been requested to adopt a pro forma (see *Part Two* of this handbook). A Best Practice note has also been issued to all court staff (again, reproduced in *Part Two*).

Welfare reports are *confidential* to the court and, in compliance with National Standards (below), should be endorsed:

> This report has been prepared for the court and should be treated as confidential. It must not be shown nor its contents revealed to any person other than a party or a legal advisor to such a party. Such legal advisor may make use of the report in connection with an application for legal aid.

The completed report is sent to the court which then releases copies to the parties' legal representatives. If a party is not legally represented then either the report is sent direct to him or her or he or she is asked to come to the court office to read it. Practice varies as to whether courts require parties to file their own statements (*Chapter 3*) before or after a welfare report is available. The statutory rules do not allow *any* statement to be filed in section 8 proceedings without a direction permitting this.

National Standards for welfare reports
National Standards set out how information should be gathered by the CWO, for example, by seeing the parties together or separately, visiting them at home, seeing the child. The standards point out that enquiries should be even-handed and fair to both parties.

Checks are made via the local authority Child Protection Register (sometimes called the 'At-risk Register'), probation records and the police.

The report should deal with all relevant matters in the 'welfare checklist' (above). In particular, the wishes and feelings of any child should be reported to the court unless there are strong grounds for not doing so, when the reasons for that should be reported. If it becomes apparent to the CWO in the course of his or her enquiries that a child may be at risk of significant harm, then this should be reported immediately to the police and social services in accordance with local child protection procedures. The court will be advised and issue directions accordingly.

CWOs make it clear to all concerned—and especially children—that their views and opinions cannot normally be withheld from the court or any of the other parties.

The report's conclusion

The conclusion in a welfare report should not be a surprise to the parties because the CWO should have kept them informed of his or her thinking. National Standards require 'a specific, reasoned recommendation where appropriate'. Case law requires courts which do not follow the recommendation of the CWO to make it clear in their stated reasons (*Chapter 3*) why they are departing from it.

Attendance of welfare officers at court

Statutory rules confirm that CWOs need not attend a court hearing or directions hearing unless ordered to do so by the court. To avoid delays, and to prevent wasteful use of CWO's time, a *Best Practice Note for the Judiciary and Family Proceedings Courts When Ordering a Welfare Report* was issued by the Children Act Advisory Committee (see *Part Two* of this handbook).

Other duties of the court welfare officer

In addition to his or her role in preparing welfare reports the CWO may be involved in family proceedings in relation to family assistance orders or supervision orders.

THE GUARDIAN AD LITEM

The need for an independent voice to speak for children in care proceedings was first recognised by the Committee of Inquiry into the death of Maria Colwell in 1974. The application to discharge the care order in that case was unopposed and the committee stated: 'It would have been of assistance to the court to have had the views of an independent social worker.'

Nowadays, in most *public law* cases, the justices' clerk or the court must appoint a *guardian ad litem* to safeguard the child's interests, unless satisfied that this is not necessary. In practice, guardians are appointed in over 98 per cent of cases.

Independence

Every local authority must maintain a panel of guardians ad litem and reporting officers (GALROs: 'reporting officers' have a function in relation to adoption: *Chapter 8*) big enough to service the requirements of the courts. Although the local authority *maintains* the panel, the member guardians are *independent* people with a social work background, most of who are self-employed. The manager of the panel must have no line responsibility for children's services within the local authority, and an independent committee advises the local authority on the appointment, dismissal and training of guardians. No-one can be appointed as a guardian if he or she is an employee of the authority involved in the case or has ever worked directly with the child or family. The regulations allow a guardian's membership of the panel to be terminated at any time if he or she is considered unsuitable or unfit. Guardians are appointed for up to three years at a time but can apply for re-appointment.

There are 54 panels in England and five in Wales (May, 1997). Although the majority consist of self-employed guardians, some areas have 'reciprocal arrangements'. These panels consist of social workers who act as guardians in, say, an adjoining county with whom a corresponding arrangement exists.

Many people believe that possible conflicts of interests and the need for the public to perceive guardians as truly independent mean that local authority involvement should cease. In 1991 the Cornwall and Isles of Scilly panel applied for judicial review of a decision by the local authority which had attempted to impose a limit on the number of hours a guardian should spend on a case. Sir Stephen Brown, President of the Family Division, said:

> I wish to emphasise how vital it is for guardians not only to be seen to be independent but also to be able to be assured themselves of their independence in the carrying out of their duties.

Role of the guardian

The guardian has a crucial role. Rule 11 FPC rules states that he or she must:

- appoint a solicitor to represent the child unless one has been appointed already
- give advice to the child according to his or her age and understanding and instruct the solicitor on all matters relevant to the interests of the child
- attend all directions appointments and hearings unless excused beforehand by the justices' clerk, panel member or court
- advise the court or justices' clerk about:
  —whether the child is of sufficient understanding to submit to examination, etc.
  —the wishes of the child generally

—the appropriate court for the hearing the proceedings
—the appropriate timing of the proceedings
—the suitability of any option being considered for the child's future
—any other matter on which the court or justices' clerk seeks his or her advice.

The guardian must also:

- notify any person, whose joining as a party might be in the child's welfare, of that person's right to apply to become a party, and inform the justices' clerk accordingly
- file a written report at least seven days before the hearing
- contact and interview such people as he or she thinks appropriate or as the court directs
- inspect such records as he or she deems appropriate. There is an absolute right to inspect local authority records; and
- obtain such professional assistance as is necessary.

During the proceedings, the guardian plays an active part through the child's solicitor. This includes briefing the solicitor with regard to questions to be asked of witnesses, and giving evidence.

Further aspects of the work of the guardian
It is worthwhile emphasising some key aspects of the guardian's work in relation to the court and the child:

- the working relationship between the guardian and the child's solicitor is a close one. Unless the solicitor feels that the child is able to give his or her own instructions, and these conflict with those of the guardian, the guardian will instruct the solicitor on all matters relevant to the interests of the child. The solicitor and guardian need to discuss and arrange such things as:
    —who should be interviewed and where
    —where the child should be seen
    —whether an expert assessment of the child is needed
  At directions appointments and court hearings the solicitor acts as the advocate for the child. Beforehand, the guardian will have worked with the solicitor to plan presentation of the child's case and will have studied the evidence, so that he or she can help the solicitor by, for example, suggesting areas for cross-examination of witnesses: see also under the heading *Separate representation*, below

- when necessary, the guardian must advise the justices' clerk or the court:
  —whether in his or her opinion the child is of sufficient understanding for any purpose, for example to consent to or to refuse medical or psychiatric examination
  —about the wishes of the child in respect of any matter. The guardian needs to remember that his or her role is limited to the court proceedings and essentially investigative and informative. The guardian is not appointed to provide therapy
- the guardian's views are relevant on allocation of the case to the appropriate court: *Chapter 3*
- the options open to the court and the suitability of each of these for the child should be put forward
- during care proceedings the guardian may discover, for example, a member of the child's extended family who is able and willing to care for the child under the auspices of a residence order. Such information should be put to the court and that person made a party to the proceedings
- the guardian must make such investigations as are necessary. This includes contacting or interviewing anyone the guardian thinks appropriate or as the court directs. The Children Act 1989 permits the guardian to inspect and take copies of local authority records and files. The guardian is also able to obtain any professional assistance which he or she thinks appropriate, or the justices' clerk or court directs. For example, the guardian may wish to seek expert advice from a child psychiatrist or a paediatrician. Although the guardian is an expert in general child care matters he or she must not purport to put himself or herself forward as an expert witness on matters about which he or she has no special knowledge, for example whether a child has been sexually abused
- it is unusual for a child to be at court but rules require the guardian to attend *all* directions hearings and court hearings unless excused by the justices' clerk or court (in contrast to the position of court welfare officers in private law proceedings: above). The guardian should advise the court if the child wishes to attend court and seek directions. Case law is generally against children attending the proceedings
- the rule that the guardian's report must be filed at least seven days before the final hearing is always subject to any other direction, as where, for example, there are genuinely unforeseen developments

- after the hearing the guardian will 'tie up the loose ends of the case'. He or she will often consult the child's solicitor to see whether an appeal is appropriate. The child needs to understand any orders made by the court and the implications for his or her future. The guardian's role is limited to the court proceedings and their immediate aftermath and the child should have been prepared for the relationship to end when the case does.

Separate representation

As already indicated, the solicitor and guardian will usually work side by side and quite amicably, but differences of opinion can arise where the child is mature enough to take a different view to the guardian and wishes to instruct the solicitor direct. The rules provide that the guardian must inform the court of any such disagreement and then act and participate in the proceedings as directed. They also provide for independent legal representation for the guardian in such a situation.

The guardian may, with the leave of the justices' clerk or the court, have legal representation 'in his or her conduct of those duties'. A difficulty is that the expense of such an appointment falls on the local authority (which must consent to it being incurred). The Children Act Advisory Committee Report for 1993/94 notes continuing concern about the possibility of a guardian becoming involved in a protracted case where he or she is separately represented. It emphasised that guardians should be eligible for legal aid in such a situation—which they are not at present.

National Standards

National Standards were published by the Department of Health and the Welsh Office in 1995. The standards confirm that:

- in each case under the Children Act 1989, the guardian ensures that the welfare of the child is the paramount consideration
- full consideration is given to ascertaining the wishes and the feelings of the child
- the guardian is professionally independent from other parties and works impartially with parents, other family members, carers and professionals at all stages of the process, subject to the need to ensure the welfare of the child
- in their work with children and families, guardians positively respond to issues associated with gender, race, culture, religion, language and disability

- the investigation is undertaken in a competent manner. Having been appointed to a particular case, the guardian constructs an initial plan setting out the intended programme and proceeds to implement it with minimum delay, updating as necessary
- where required by statute, the guardian's investigation incorporates the welfare checklist
- having brought together the relevant information, the guardian evaluates it and makes judgements about what future arrangements will be in the best interests of the child; whether any order is needed, and *if it is* whether the order sought is the one most likely to achieve the child's best interests
- the guardian's report accords with both national and local guidelines on report writing
- the guardian attends relevant directions appointments in accordance with the court rules, and is prepared for each court hearing
- prior to closing the case, guardians ensure that they have considered appropriate actions and if necessary carried them out in respect of the child
- the guardian works within the agreed objectives, policies, standards and procedures of the service as approved by the panel committee.

Quite independently of National Standards, the National Association for GALROs has a code of ethics for members. Each panel of guardians should have an appraisal system to ensure that a high standard of reports is maintained.

A NOTE ON MEDICAL REPORTS

The Children Act Advisory Committee in its 1994/95 *Annual Report* considered whether, and if so how, medical reports prepared for cases involving children should be released to the child's GP so as to be included in the child's medical records. It was felt that the court may have before it important information on the child's physical or mental condition which could assist other people concerned with the child's health on a day-to-day basis. As any documents prepared for the court are confidential and cannot normally be released, court welfare officers or guardians ad litem should, if appropriate, raise this question with the court at the conclusion of any proceedings. The Children Act Advisory Committee recommended the following practice:

- in every case in which a medical report on a child is made consideration should be given to the desirability of releasing the report, or information from it, to the child's GP
- where there are conflicting reports, or where the court's finding conflicts with the opinion of the expert (e.g. whether the child has been sexually abused), the question of whether the report, or reports, or extracts should be released to the GP should be raised as an issue
- it should be borne in mind that reports may contain information given by third parties in confidence, and the court's attention should be drawn to this when it is invited to make an order for release
- in any event, the leave of the court should be sought to release relevant information to the child's GP, either to assist in current or proposed treatment, or as part of the confidential records of the child's medical history
- if the child has the capacity to make decisions with regard to treatment his or her consent to the release of the information must also be obtained.

AVOIDING MISUSE OF THE PROVISIONS

Early Children Act Advisory Committee reports identified misuse of the power which exists under section 37 Children Act 1989 for a court in *private law* proceedings to require a local authority to investigate the circumstances of a child (see above) so as to bring about the involvement of a guardian ad litem in those proceedings. However, properly used, the existence the power to direct an investigation can ensure that the court is able to act in the best interests of a child, having the benefit of the fullest possible relevant information.

CHAPTER 5

Financial Provision

Family proceedings courts deal with applications for financial provision by *parties to a marriage* (sometimes called 'pecuniary orders')—but now only to a limited extent with maintenance for *children*, since the Child Support Agency (CSA) was given this responsibility. The court *does* deal with the variation of court orders for the maintenance of children which pre-date the present system, although the CSA is gradually 'taking over' these matters.

APPLICATIONS BY SPOUSES

Divorce settlements are made only in the High Court and county court. As mentioned in *Chapter 6*, these orders can be registered in the magistrates' court for enforcement. But if someone wishes to obtain maintenance from their spouse whilst they remain married to each other, application can *only* be made to the family proceedings court. The relevant law affecting such applications is contained in the Domestic Proceedings and Magistrates' Courts Act 1978 and associated procedures in the Family Proceedings Courts (Matrimonial Proceedings etc.) Rules 1991. The main types of orders are:

- section 2 orders—on one or more of the 'fault-based' grounds set out below
- section 6 applications on the basis of agreement; and
- section 7 orders—sometimes called 'living apart' orders.

In the absence of an admission (or with section 6 orders 'agreement') by the other party, the burden is on the applicant to establish a ground to the civil standard of proof, i.e. on a balance of probabilities.

SECTION 2 ORDERS

Either party to a marriage may apply under Section 2 of the 1978 Act for an order based on one or more of the grounds listed below, i.e. that the other party to the marriage ('the respondent') has:

- *failed to provide reasonable maintenance for the applicant* Until 1978 failure had to be 'wilful', but this is no longer the case. The

71

respondent's motives are irrelevant. The question is the straightforward one of whether reasonable maintenance has been provided. The test is an objective one.

- *failed to provide, or make a proper contribution towards, reasonable maintenance for any child of the family* Once this ground is established the *applicant* can obtain an order in *his or her own* favour even though the failure is proved only in respect of a child of the family, meaning:
    —a child of both parties to the marriage; or
    —any other child (not being a child placed with the parties as foster parents) who has been *treated* by both parties as a child of the family.

This ground remains despite the Child Support Act 1991. There are also some other exceptions to the general rule that child maintenance is dealt with by the CSA. Magistrates should seek legal advice if asked to make an order for a child.

- *behaved in such a way that the applicant cannot reasonably be expected to live with the respondent* This basis is usually referred to as 'unreasonable behaviour'. Rulings of the higher courts indicate that in divorce cases—where the same ground applies—the approach is to ask:

> Would any right thinking person come to the conclusion that this husband has behaved in such a way that this wife cannot reasonably be expected to live with him, taking into account the whole of the circumstances and the characters and personalities of the parties?

The test is thus partly objective (what a 'reasonable person' might say) and partly subjective (i.e. taking account of the individual 'characters and personalities of the parties'). Usually, the application will contain a brief statement of the behaviour which is alleged to be unreasonable. Case law indicates that when adultery is relied on as a basis for unreasonable behaviour, details of the allegation should be given.

- *deserted the applicant* The applicant will need to prove:
    —that cohabitation between the parties has ended
    —that this is intentional on the part of the 'deserter'
    —that the party alleging desertion has not consented to the separation.

Cohabitation does not necessarily mean, for example, living in the same house. A husband might work abroad or elsewhere with the express or implied agreement of his wife. What matters is the parties' intentions. Neither does desertion have to be for any specific length of time—and it is deemed to be at an end if the 'deserter' makes a *bona fide* offer to return which the deserted party could reasonably be expected to accept. Refusal of such an offer might be reasonable, for example, where there is a history of domestic violence.

Constructive desertion: a note There is a form of desertion known as 'constructive desertion'. This occurs where the party alleging that he or she has been deserted is the one who has left the other party, but claims that he or she was forced into this by the other party's conduct.

Any order made should say which ground or grounds is or are proved, and, if desertion is a ground, when it began.

Financial orders which can be made
Once the applicant proves a 'section 2' ground the court can make one or more of the following forms of financial provision, i.e. an order for:

- *periodical payments*   These may be weekly, monthly or by reference to any other period which is convenient in a given case
- *a lump sum* A lump sum cannot exceed £1000 (May, 1997). However, it can be ordered to be paid by instalments.

Children
In those exceptional cases where children are not 'qualifying children' within the meaning of the Child Support Act 1991 (seek legal advice), the court can order:

- *periodical payments* to or for the benefit of a child
- *a lump sum* for the benefit of a child, or to the child direct. A lump sum cannot exceed £1,000 (May, 1997).

No order can be made in respect of a child aged 18 years or over unless he or she is at an educational establishment or undergoing training for a trade, profession or vocation, whether or not also in work, or where there are special circumstances.

In relation to section 2 applications involving requests for orders in respect of children under 18 years of age the court cannot make a final order or dismiss the application before deciding whether to exercise any of the powers available under the Children Act 1989: see *Chapter 2*.

Duration of section 2 orders

The order must be for a term fixed by the court—but can, for example, be for 'the joint lives of the parties'). Whatever the term, it must be specified in the order. The term cannot:

- begin earlier than the date when the application was made (i.e. it *can* be backdated to that time); or
- extend beyond the death of either party.

If the parties subsequently divorce and the order remains in force because not superseded by an order of the divorce court, then it ceases on remarriage by the party entitled to payments. Any arrears due at that time remain payable and enforceable: see, generally, *Chapter 6*.

If other proceedings—such as divorce proceedings —take place at a later date in either the High Court or county court, that court may order that the magistrates' court order shall cease on a specified date. This does not apply to orders for lump sums.

Children

The same basic principles concerning the duration of periodical payments orders apply as for adults, subject to the following rules:

- the order should not, in the first instance, extend beyond the child's seventeenth birthday, unless the welfare of the child requires this, or the circumstances are as already described above in relation to education, training or special circumstances—when the order can be made to run until, or be continued beyond, 18 years of age
- the order is not affected by remarriage
- an order for a child ceases automatically on the death of the person liable to make the payments.

AGREED ORDERS (SECTION 6)

Under section 6 of the 1978 Act, either party to a marriage can apply for an order for financial provision if the other party has agreed to make the provision set out in the application. The rules concerning the duration of agreed orders, their cessation and application to children mirror those for section 2 orders above, i.e. agreement must be within the same parameters.

The court does not simply 'rubber stamp' agreements. It must consider the proposal and have no reason to think that the suggested order will be contrary to the interests of justice. In respect of agreed orders to or for the benefit of children (which can only be made in the same limited circumstances mentioned in relation to section 2 orders, above) the court must also be satisfied that the order, if made, will make a proper contribution towards the financial needs of the child.

There can be an application for a section 6 order at any time before a section 2 order is made, in effect the parties can 'switch' to a section 6 agreed order—as where agreement is reached after proceedings have been launched, or following mediation (below). The earlier application is then treated as withdrawn.

LIVING APART ORDERS (SECTION 7)

'Living apart' applications are quite rare. Parties to a marriage who:

- have been living apart for a continuous period exceeding three months
- neither having deserted the other (see *Section 2 Orders*, above); and
- where one of the parties has been making periodical payments

can apply for an order for financial provision under section 7. The application must give details of the aggregate payment in the three months immediately preceding the date when the application was made. The court must be satisfied that the respondent has made the payments stated. If the court feels that the amount would not provide reasonable maintenance for the applicant, or a proper contribution for a child of the family (in the limited cases where there is power to order such provision: see above), then the court can refuse to make the order and treat it as if it had been made under section 2, i.e. on the basis of failure to provide reasonable maintenance.

The rules concerning the duration of living apart orders, their automatic cessation and application to children mirror those for section 2 orders above.

THE AMOUNT OF THE ORDER ('QUANTUM')

There are two stages to proceedings involving financial provision:

- establishing whether a ground exists for an order (or agreement); and

- assessing the amount of periodical payments and lump sum orders—and deciding on their timing. This second stage also applies to agreed orders and living apart orders in the sense that the court can intervene, as described in relation to those orders.

The matters which courts must have regard to are listed in the 1978 Act. They must also have regard to *all* the circumstances of the case, first consideration being given to the welfare while a minor of any child of the family who has not attained the age of 18. Under section 3, the court must have regard, in particular, to the following items when determining *spouse maintenance:*

(a) the income, earning capacity, property and other financial resources which each of the parties to the marriage has or is likely to have in the foreseeable future, including in the case of earning capacity any increase in the capacity which it would in the opinion of the court be reasonable to expect a party to the marriage to take steps to acquire;
(b) the financial needs, obligations and responsibilities which each of the parties to the marriage has or is likely to have in the foreseeable future;
(c) the standard of living enjoyed by the parties to the marriage before the occurrence of the conduct which is alleged as the ground of the application;
(d) the age of each party to the marriage and the duration of the marriage;
(e) any physical or mental disability of either of the parties to the marriage;
(f) the contributions which each of the parties has made or is likely in the foreseeable future to make to the welfare of the family, including any contributions by looking after the home or caring for the family;
(g) the conduct of each of the parties, if that conduct is such that it would in the opinion of the court be inequitable to disregard it.

The court must have regard to the following items, in particular, if determining *child maintenance:*

(a) the financial needs of the child;
(b) the income, earning capacity (if any), property and other financial resources of the child;
(c) any physical or mental disability of the child;
(d) the standard of living enjoyed by the family before the occurrence of the conduct which is alleged as the ground of the application;
(e) the manner in which the child was being and in which the parties to the marriage expected him to be educated or trained;
(f) the matters mentioned in relation to the parties to the marriage in paragraphs (a) or (b) above.

Before exercising powers in favour of a child of the family who is not a child of the respondent, the court must have regard:

(a) to whether the respondent had assumed any responsibility for the child's maintenance and, if he did, to the extent to which, and the basis on which, he assumed that responsibility and to the length of time during which, he discharge that responsibility;

(b) to whether in assuming and discharging that responsibility the respondent did so knowing that the child was not his own child;

(c) to the liability of any other person to maintain the child.

Applying the statutory criteria

Various decided cases set out 'formulae' to assist courts in assessing the amount of maintenance, for example the so-called 'one third rule' which involves adding together the gross incomes of both parties, dividing by three, subtracting the wife's gross earnings, and treating the balance as a starting point to which the statutory criteria can then be applied. This and other methods used by courts attracted criticism in that they can produce anomalies and uncertainty. It was criticism of the 'discretionary approach' of the courts that led to the introduction of a 'formula' to be applied across the board in most child maintenance cases by the Child Support Agency.

Some specific factors affecting financial provision

There are two frequently recurring items on which the law offers guidance:

Second wife, mistress or consort

Whichever starting point a court uses, it will often be necessary to decide to what extent obligations to support—or the resources of a second wife or cohabitee—should be brought into account in determining a man's liability to maintain a former wife. The *resources* of a second wife or mistress cannot be taken into account when applying the statutory criteria (above). That provision refers only to the income etc. of *the parties to the marriage*. However, such resources may be relevant if the result is that *more* of a former husband's income is freed for the payment of maintenance to his first wife and their children. Conversely, a second relationship may mean that a man has *less* resources. The High Court has held that a man *can* have financial responsibility for his cohabitee and her child. There is nothing in the statutory criteria which restricts the range of obligations and responsibilities to those which are legally enforceable.

Unemployment

Where a party is in receipt of benefits, the court should take into account that the Department of Social Security must have accepted that he or she is genuinely unable to obtain employment. However, although a weighty factor, the payment of benefit and the fact that this is continuing is *not conclusive* evidence that someone is unable to obtain work or is unemployed if, for example, the other party produces clear evidence that he or she is working whilst drawing benefits. Where someone *is* genuinely unemployed, a 'nominal order' is usually made.

INTERIM ORDERS

If a married couple separate, the applicant may need maintenance urgently. Where an application is made under any of sections 2, 6 or 7 above, the court can make an interim order. The interim order cannot commence before the date of the application and ceases on whichever of the following dates occurs first:

- the date specified in the order; or
- three months from the date the order was made; or
- the date when the court makes a final order or dismisses the case.

There is power to extend interim orders for *one* further three month period, making six months in all.

ORDERS FOR PAYMENT

When a court makes an order for periodical payments, it can order payment to be made:

- direct between the parties
- to the clerk of the court, or the clerk of any other magistrates' court (in his or her role as 'collecting officer')
- by standing order or any other method which requires payments to be made from one account to another
- as arranged by the secretary of state
- by attachment of earnings order (i.e. an employer will deduct a given amount at regular intervals and forward this to the court: the principles are then comparable to those in relation to enforcement: *Chapter 6*).

CASE MANAGEMENT

Although there is no statutory system of allocation (as there is in relation to Children Act proceedings), where an application has been made under section 2 of the 1978 Act, the court may refuse to deal with it if it believes that it would be more conveniently dealt with by the High Court.

Some key procedures
The Family Proceedings Courts (Matrimonial Proceedings etc.) Rules 1991 state, amongst other things that:

- prescribed forms must be used
- 21 days notice must be given
- within the next 14 days the respondent must file and serve on the parties an 'answer' to the application
- directions for the conduct of the proceedings can be given, varied or revoked by the court or the justices' clerk
- each party must file a statement with the court setting out the substance of his or her evidence; and
- the magistrates' reasons must be recorded and announced in court.

RECONCILIATION

When a ground based application for financial provision is under consideration pursuant to section 2 (above)—and before finally proceeding to a hearing or exercising powers to make orders—the court must always consider whether there is any possibility of a *reconciliation* between the parties. The case can be adjourned at any stage if it seems that there is a reasonable prospect of this and the court can ask the court welfare officer to assist the parties in a similar way to that described in *Chapter 4*. The officer will then report to the court on whether or not the attempt at reconciliation has been successful.

VARIATION, REVOCATION AND REVIVAL

Once an order is in force an application can be made to vary its provisions or to revoke it altogether. The court has power to temporarily suspend an order for periodical payments. In some circumstances it is possible to revive an order which has ceased to have effect (seek legal advice).

The court must give effect to any agreement reached by the parties so far as it appears just to do so. When dealing with variation applications, orders to which the respondent consents can be made without hearing evidence. If there is no agreement, the court must have regard to all the circumstances of the case, including any changes in the application of the statutory criteria.

Variation in the method of payment
The court can also order a variation in the *method* of payment. This can be on application by either party, or, if payments have not been made as ordered, the court can review the situation and order payment by any of the methods described under the heading *Orders for Payment* above.

Revival where the child is over 16 years of age
If an order for a child ceases between the age of 16 and 18 years, he or she may apply to the court for its revival at any time up until his or her eighteenth birthday.

THE CHILD SUPPORT AGENCY

As emphasised at the start of this chapter, the family proceedings court generally no longer has responsibility for child maintenance. The Child Support Act 1991 introduced a formula approach under the auspices of the Child Support Agency (CSA) and—since 1993—the CSA has had the task of assessing and collecting maintenance for children. There are exceptions to this, but the vast bulk of child maintenance is now dealt with by the CSA. The CSA works out what child maintenance should be paid and by whom. The resulting figure is then reviewed annually and there is also a review if either parent's circumstances change. Child support is enforceable by the agency through the magistrates' court (in practice the family proceedings court in most areas): *Chapter 6.*

The formula and 'departures'
Despite the fact that the CSA was set up partly because it was felt that courts—having a discretion as to the amount of maintenance—acted inconsistently, one of the major criticisms of the new formula approach was its inflexibility, which many fathers felt caused injustice. In April 1995, amendments tried to deal with two aspects of this: first, the lack of any allowance for high travel costs to work; and second, the situation where there had been previous agreements to transfer property. The 1991 Act was changed to allow for 'departures' from the formula. Corresponding regulations were applied to several pilot areas—and extended to all areas in 1996.

Old cases and transfer to the CSA
As at 1993, courts were administering a large number of maintenance orders. The CSA is scheduled to take over these cases. The law requires it

to notify the court holding the original order immediately a fresh CSA assessment in respect of the child is made. From that time onwards the court order ceases and the CSA has jurisdiction. The court is still under a duty to enforce any arrears existing at the time of the case being taken over. Regulations allow a child support officer to cancel such an assessment if it transpires that the assessment was made in error. The court is notified of the cancellation and the court order is then revived.

The original schedule was for all existing orders to be taken over by the CSA by April, 1997—but the timetable has not been adhered to and there is, at the time of writing (May, 1997), no specific time within which the CSA will complete these transitional arrangements. Until they *are* taken over, or revoked by the court, the family proceedings court retains jurisdiction over existing court orders.

New applications
In respect of new applications, when parties separate the CSA *requires* a parent with care who is receiving income support, family credit, disability working allowance or income based jobseeker's allowance to apply to the CSA. Parents with care who are not receiving benefits etc. *may* apply to the CSA, unless they have an existing court order for maintenance.

Declarations of parentage
Normally, when the CSA receives an application the child support officer cannot make an assessment if the person alleged to be a parent of the child denies this. However, the CSA itself, or (less frequently) the person with care of the child, may apply to the family proceedings court for a declaration of parentage against the alleged parent—who becomes the respondent.

At the hearing, the respondent is asked if he or she admits being a parent. If so, a declaration of parentage is made. The CSA is then able to complete the maintenance assessment. If the respondent denies being a parent of the child, the court must resolved this issue by way of a hearing. At the request of the CSA or the alleged parent, the court may make a direction for blood tests pursuant to the Family Law Reform Act 1969: see *Blood Tests*, below.

FINANCIAL PROVISION UNDER THE CHILDREN ACT 1989

Applications for financial provision in respect of children—when not 'attached' to a parent's application and if not excluded by the terms of the Child Support Act 1991 (the usual position)—must be made under the Children Act 1989, section 15 and schedule 1. These are deemed to be 'family proceedings'. Applications can be made by any:

- parent
- guardian
- other person who holds a residence order in respect of a child.

There will normally be a specific application but—on making, varying or discharging a residence order—the court can make a financial order for the child even though no application has been made.

A magistrates' court can order periodical payments or a lump sum of up to £1000 to either an applicant for the benefit of the child, or to the child. Either or both of the parents can be ordered to pay.

Matters to which court must have regard
The court must consider all the circumstances of the case, including statutory criteria analogous to those described in relation to orders under the Domestic Proceedings and Magistrates' Courts Act 1978 above: see under the heading *The Amount of the Order ('Quantum')*.

Procedures
The Children Act procedures described in *Chapter 3* apply equally to this variety of application. The applicant starts by filing a 'Form C1' with the court, together with supplement (C10A), which includes a statement of means. Within 14 days of service of the application, a respondent must acknowledge receipt and give relevant information.

Duration of orders
The order can be backdated but cannot be made to start earlier than the date of the application and should not extend, in the first instance, beyond the child's seventeenth birthday, unless a later date, which should not be beyond the child's eighteenth birthday, is appropriate. An order can only go beyond 18 years of age if the child is receiving education or training or there are special circumstances. It ceases to have effect on the death of the payer or if the parents live together for more than six months.

Variation, discharge, suspension and revival
On an application to vary or discharge periodical payments, the court must have regard to all the circumstances of the case, including any change to the matters to which the court originally had to have regard (above). The court is able to temporarily suspend provision and revive it.

An order can be revived on application by the child between the ages of 16 and 18.

Interim orders

At any time before the court disposes of the application it can make an interim order. This cannot start before the date of the application and ceases when the full application is dealt with, or on the date specified in the interim order, if earlier.

BLOOD TESTS

Blood tests are generally accepted as being the best evidence whether or not a man is the natural father of a child. Such tests are to be preferred to oral evidence about the parties sexual liaisons. Magistrates must be satisfied—on a balance of probabilities—that the alleged parent is the parent of the child before an order or declaration is made. Obviously, if blood tests *are* taken and show that a man alleged to be the father of a child is excluded from paternity, then the applicant or CSA will withdraw the application.

The Family Law Reform Act 1969 and the Magistrates' Courts (Blood Tests) Rules 1971 set out the procedures. The application can be made orally at the hearing or in writing at any time. If both parties agree, the court can give a direction for blood tests before the first hearing.

If the parties to the application consent to the blood being taken from them and the child the procedure is as follows:

- the court gives the direction for the use of blood tests
- a period is specified in the direction (normally six to ten weeks), during which the blood is to be taken from the parties and child and tested
- the court must ascertain who is to pay for the tests (the total cost being around £500). This will usually be the applicant; and
- a report is obtained from the tester.

If the applicant is legally aided, then often the certificate will cover the cost of the blood tests. If not, the applicant will need funds to pay for tests before the court will make the arrangements. When the CSA applies for a declaration of parentage it will usually agree to pay the costs but seek to recover them from the respondent if the tests ultimately reveal that he is the father.

Ordering blood tests is an important matter and involves an exercise in judicial discretion. If one of the parties does not consent to blood samples being taken, the court must decide whether or not to make the direction.

In *Re H (Paternity Blood Test)* 1996 2 FLR 65 the mother opposed the use of blood tests but the judge nevertheless made a direction. On appeal, it was held that although the mother's refusal was a factor to be taken into account, it could not be determinative. It was indicated that although the welfare of the child did not dominate matters, a court should not order a blood test if it would be against the child's interests. In looking at those interests, it was pointed out that in cases—for example, where there is a husband and 'father' of the child but a man with whom the wife has had an affair claims to be the father—disturbance to the child's security must be weighed against the loss to the child of the certainty of knowing who he or she is. Every child has a right to know the truth unless his or her welfare clearly justifies a 'cover up'. It was stated that honesty is the best policy, and that biological parentage should be divorced from psychological parentage.

Such inferences as appear proper in the circumstances can be drawn if a party refuses consent to a blood test or to comply with a direction that samples be taken. In *Re H* above it was pointed out that a refusal to allow for the virtual 'certainty' that DNA testing provides would normally justify some inference that a refusal was to hide the truth—and it was suggested that this inference would be even stronger if a court direction was flouted.

REGISTERED ORDERS

Orders made in the High Court or county court are paid direct between the parties. If the payer fails to make payments the person entitled to payments can apply to the court which made the order—pursuant to the Maintenance Orders Act 1958—to register the maintenance order for enforcement in a magistrates' court. If granted, the 'registered order' is sent to the magistrates' court which is local to where the payer resides and is registered there. It can then be enforced as if made in that court: *Chapter 6.*

Registered orders can also be varied by a magistrates' court—in fact the 1958 Act provides that the rate of payment shall not be varied *except* by the court of registration or some other magistrates' court. However, the case can be remitted to the original court during a variation hearing if appropriate. The magistrates' court is only allowed to vary or alter the rate of payment. If, for example, an application is made to extend the order this must be dealt with by the High Court or county court. Once the application *is* before the High Court or county court then that court can also vary the rate of payment.

CHAPTER 6

Enforcement

There are inevitably cases where parties are unable or unwilling to comply with court orders. The most common situation involves the payment of money under one of those orders for financial provision described in *Chapter 5*. In relation to cases under the Children Act 1989 as dealt with in *Chapter 2*, seemingly the most frequent situation in which enforcement becomes an issue is when the party with care or residence and a party with contact disagree. Different rules apply depending upon whether the original order involves:

- payment of money (*financial* or *pecuniary* orders); or
- doing or failing to do something other than the payment of money, such as allowing contact in the terms laid down by the court. In relation to this type of order it is necessary to consider
  —magistrates' general powers of enforcement in *civil cases*; and
  —a number of special powers designed for particular situations.

The ultimate sanction in relation to both types of order is committal to custody, albeit under different rules. Such action is heavily circumscribed by law and used sparingly in practice—as a last resort after considering all other options, and following legal advice. Failure to seek, or act upon, proper advice can render magistrates personally liable.

CHILD AND OTHER NON-FINANCIAL ORDERS

Enforcement proceedings are rarely a satisfactory answer in cases concerning children. The ultimate sanction of imprisonment prevents contact between the child and the party concerned, and any penalising, say, of a parent can have negative effects vis-à-vis that relationship and the child's welfare. It is unlikely to provide a positive climate in which to bring up the child. More subtle and informal methods may be needed—such as the use of a trained counsellor or mediation. Nonetheless, when all else fails it may be necessary to rely on statutory powers.

Section 63 Magistrates Courts Act 1980
Section 63 contains the main general enforcement powers in civil cases. These are *specifically excluded* in respect of orders for the payment of money (below) and in certain other situations: seek legal advice. The

injured party must normally apply for a summons. Proceedings for alleged breach of a residence order differ in that a statement must also be filed (below). Section 63(3) provides:

> where any person disobeys an order of a magistrates' court . . : to do anything other than the payment of money or to abstain from doing anything the court may:
> (a) order him to pay a sum not exceeding £50 for every day during which he is in default or a sum not exceeding £5000; or
> (b) commit him to custody until he has remedied his default or for a period not exceeding two months;
> but a person who is ordered to pay a sum for every day during which he is in default or is committed to custody until he has remedied his default shall not by virtue of this section be ordered to pay more than £1000 or be committed for more than two months in all for doing or abstaining from doing the same thing, contrary to the order.

The Children Act Advisory Committee expressed the view that section 63(3) could not apply to non-compliance with directions given by a justices' clerk or a single magistrate as the provision only applies to orders of a *court*.

The breach
The summons will recite the order and state in what way it is alleged to have been disobeyed. It should include such matters as the time, place and date of the alleged breach. Before the court can consider taking action it needs to be satisfied that there has been deliberate and wilful disobedience of the order. The justices' clerk or legal advisor must make a note of the evidence, since appeal may follow to the High Court. That court has repeatedly stated that committal to custody is to be viewed as a last resort and—in *family proceedings*—as a *very last* resort. Such an order:

> . . . should be made very reluctantly and only . . . when every other method to bring the situation under control has failed, or is almost certain to fail.

No power to suspend
Whilst there is no power to suspend the operation of a committal under section 63, a party may decide to comply with the order after being committed to custody. In these circumstances 'the contempt will be purged' and he or she will be set free.

Contact
Generally speaking, declaratory orders (i.e. declaring what a party's rights are) are *not* enforceable by way of committal. However, the

Children Act 1989 ensures that a contact order is an order *requiring* someone to do something.

If there is non-compliance or disagreement, consideration should be given to one or both parties seeking a 'defined order'. This will set out in precise terms the contact requirements. The higher courts have proffered advice on the question of enforcing access (the predecessor to contact) and this, in the main, is still relevant:

> The object of the exercise is to enforce the order for access in the sense of getting it working or putting something more workable in its place. This is rarely achieved by sending a parent to prison or by fining them. Indeed, the odds are that such an approach will only serve to aggravate the hostility that already may exist between the parties.

Magistrates should try to discover why contact has not taken place as ordered and, if appropriate, explore the possibility of a variation of the order so that the terms are acceptable to *both* parties. In this context, it is important that the original order is realistic.

The Court of Appeal stated in 1996 that courts have powers to enforce orders for contact, which they should not hesitate to use where it is judged that this will, overall, promote the welfare of the child. However:

> cases did, unhappily and infrequently but occasionally arise in which a court was compelled to conclude that in existing circumstances an order for immediate direct contact should not be ordered, because so to order would injure the welfare of the child.

In Re H (Contact: Enforcement) (1996) 1 FLR 614 is illustrative of other constraints. A contact order set out the date and time when a child was to be handed over, but did not state where. The mother failed to hand the child over and the father proceeded under section 63. The mother appealed against being fined. It was held that:

- the original failure to define the place where the child was to be handed over was fatal to any application under section 63
- the wife had not deliberately flouted the order
- section 63 was an inappropriate way to enforce a contact order unless there was no realistic alternative.

Comparison with other courts

In the High Court or county court an order may be enforceable as an injunction, and where an undertaking by a party (see the example reproduced in *Part Two* of this handbook) is incorporated in an order of the court that may be enforceable in the same way. To be enforceable by committal (in the case of those courts via their power to punish a party for contempt), the injunction or undertaking must set out in explicit terms what it is that the party in question must do, or must refrain from doing. Where the order or undertaking requires someone to do an act, it will only be enforceable if the order or undertaking also specifies the time within which the act is to be done.

Consequently, a general form of order, such as that a child is to have contact with a party, cannot be enforced by committal: see *D v D (Access: contempt: committal)* (1991) 2 FLR 34. To be enforceable it must specify when, and where (*In re H*, above) the child is to be allowed contact, as well as with whom. Furthermore, if an order is made in the nature of an injunction in the county court it will not be enforceable unless it has attached to it a 'penal notice' which tells the person to whom it is addressed that if the order *is* disobeyed he or she may be punished by being committed to prison. The same principles would apply equally to any other form of order, for example a prohibited steps order.

Residence orders
The Children Act 1989 (in conjunction with the general enforcement powers in section 63 Magistrates' Courts Act 1980: above) enables magistrates to consider an alleged breach of a residence order—provided that the person in whose favour the order was made files a *written statement* describing the alleged breach. A residence order may then be enforced as if it were an order requiring the other person to produce the child to the person in whose favour the order was made.

Family Law Act 1986
The 1986 Act provides that when enforcing section 8 orders:

- the court may order any person who it has reason to believe may have relevant information about the whereabouts of a child to disclose that information
- where there is an order to give up a child to another person and a court is satisfied that the child has not been given up in accordance with that order, the court can make an order authorising an officer of the court or a constable to take charge of the child and deliver him or her to the person concerned.

Legal opinion differs as to whether county court or High Court residence orders can be enforced in magistrates' courts. Most legal advisors appear to consider that the magistrates' jurisdiction to enforce is limited to enforcing their *own orders.*

ALTERNATIVE MODES OF ENFORCEMENT

Some orders made by the family panel are *not* enforceable as such, or enforcement takes the form of criminal proceedings.

Breach of a care order would not be the subject of action under section 63 but, in appropriate circumstances, a recovery order could be obtained (*Chapter 2*). There are criminal offences of abduction and of obstructing anyone attempting to enforce such an order.

If a supervision order is 'breached', the supervisor would be well advised to consider whether there should be an application for the variation or discharge of that order. In appropriate circumstances a care order will need to be considered. In respect of an education supervision order, a criminal prosecution of the parents could follow for persistently failing to comply with a direction under the order. In practice, the local authority would be asked to make enquiries and this could result in *public law* proceedings for a care or supervision order.

Enforcement of magistrates' orders in other courts
If associated proceedings are pending in the High Court or county court, the family proceedings court should not hear any proposed enforcement proceedings in relation to one of its existing orders: seek legal advice.

FINANCIAL ORDERS

Magistrates' court maintenance orders and certain other financial orders (including High Court and county court orders registered in magistrates' courts) are enforceable as described in this section. Child support resulting from an assessment by the Child Support Agency has a separate enforcement mechanism: below. The object of enforcement is to seek compliance with the order, not to punish the defaulter. The orders available to courts in enforcement proceedings are:

- payment by standing order
- distress (i.e. ordering goods to be seized by bailiffs or court officers and sold, and the proceeds paid over for transmission to the person entitled to the money). Distress can be postponed
- attachment of earnings; and
- imprisonment (immediate or suspended on terms).

The original order
The family proceedings court will have ordered payment by one of the following methods:

- direct to the payee
- via the court office (the 'collecting office')
- by standing order
- attachment of earnings.

The collecting office
The department of the court administration which deals with maintenance payments is called the 'collecting office'. Maintenance payments in family proceedings before magistrates are usually made through the justices' clerk, who, by virtue of his office as clerk to the justices is also designated 'collecting officer' (although this responsibility can nowadays be held, say, centrally in a county, or as explained in *Chapter 1*). He or she also has a duty to comply with relevant statutory provisions concerning maintenance payments, their collection and enforcement. This includes, for example, notifying the payee when arrears are due under the order.

Interim orders and costs
Interim orders are enforceable in the same way as final orders. Costs are also enforceable in the same way as maintenance payments.

Death or discharge
In general, the death of either party in respect of a maintenance order will result in the power to enforce ceasing. An order discharged for some other reason can still be enforced if arrears are outstanding.

Action by the collecting officer
When an order is in arrears, the collecting officer may take proceedings against the payer *with the authority of the payee* unless he or she considers it unreasonable in the circumstances. Sometimes, in fact, the payee will not give authority. Furthermore, the clerk's authority to enforce may be withdrawn by the payee at any stage by giving notice in writing.

The payee may also bring proceedings in his or her own name. This may be necessary where the collecting officer refuses to take proceedings on the payee's behalf.

Commencement of enforcement proceedings
Enforcement proceedings are started by making a complaint (often called an 'application'). This cannot occur earlier than the fifteenth day after the order. Either a summons or a warrant will be issued. Before a warrant can be issued, the complaint must be substantiated on oath—and a good reason will need to be put forward and be accepted as to why a summons will not suffice.

Not 'family proceedings'

Enforcement proceedings are not automatically designated 'family proceedings'—and hence they can be heard in any adult magistrates' court. However, good practice suggests that in the majority of cases they should be designated family proceedings by order of the court. If this happens, they will be heard by the family proceedings court and, for example, provisions such as press restrictions (*Chapter 3*) will apply.

Which arrears?

The practice is to enforce only arrears which have accrued within the year before the date of the start of the enforcement proceedings. Normally the complaint will be issued for the full amount of the arrears and the court will consider remitting any balance dating from more than 12 months ago. In a leading case, a wife had failed to enforce an order for a number of years. The justices declined to remit any arrears and on appeal were criticised and remission ordered. The High Court said that only arrears which had accrued in the year before the complaint was made should be enforced.

Means inquiry

The court must inquire into the means of the defaulter—who is usually asked to complete a written statement of means before taking the witness stand. He or she will be asked, on oath or affirmation, to confirm the contents of the statement and various supplementary questions will be put to the defaulter—normally by the court legal advisor, who will have the account details and case file—so that the magistrates are not drawn 'into the arena'. Such questioning can be in the nature of cross-examination. The magistrates' normally ask any residual questions 'by way of clarification' or to cover items which they consider to be particularly relevant. An employer can be directed to supply a statement of wages. The magistrates, of course, carry out the adjudication process, with legal advice as necessary.

Means report

A probation officer may be directed to prepare a report on the means of either or both parties and present this in writing or orally. If so, either party or the court can require the probation officer to attend to give evidence.

Venue

This is normally the court which made the order. However, where the complainant resides in a different petty sessions area and payment is directed there, that court may hear the complaint for arrears. Similarly, where the defaulter is for the time being in a different area, the complaint can be sent there for enforcement. That court will then issue the summons or warrant—and non-payment is proved by a certificate from the collecting officer to whom payments should have been made. Special provisions (beyond the scope of this handbook) exist for enforcing orders from abroad in England and Wales and vice-versa, known as 'reciprocal enforcement'.

Attendance at court

The *payee* (as opposed to the *defaulter*) need not attend arrears proceedings where process has been initiated in the name of the collecting officer—and normally does not do so unless, possibly, remission is in prospect or payments are alleged to have been made direct to the payee. Sometimes a 'cross-application' to vary the order is heard at the same time as a complaint for arrears, when both parties will need to be present at court.

Power to search

The court can direct that the defaulter be searched. If cash is found in his or her possession, the court can apply this to the order unless the court is satisfied that the money does not belong to him or her or that the loss of it would be more injurious to his or her family than detention.

Costs

The court has a discretion to order such costs as it thinks just and reasonable. In practice, costs are rarely ordered because this reduces any potential to make maintenance payments.

Adjournment

This may occur for a variety of reasons. It can be to monitor proposed payments by the defaulter—it might be to allow for a variation application where the defaulter's circumstances have altered since the original order was made. It can be to give the payee an opportunity to attend where remission is under consideration (below). When a case is adjourned there is no power to remand the defaulter and the Bail Act 1976 is inapplicable.

Remission

The court has power to remit (i.e. cancel out) all or part of any arrears. This power extends to High Court and county court orders registered for collection via the magistrates' court. It was reiterated in *R v Bristol Magistrates' Court, ex parte Hodge* (1997) 1 FLR 88 that it is mandatory that the court must notify the payee of its intention to consider remission. It has been held that a general permission of the payee in the notice of the enforcement proceedings will not suffice. It is thus common practice for the payee to be given written notice with the reasons for the court's proposal stated in it. The payee is usually given the choice of making a written response or attending the hearing to make personal representations. The power to remit must be exercised judicially. In one case where a wife impeded access to children, it was held that the purported remission was improper.

Good practice suggests that any arrears older than 12 months should be remitted in any event (see *Which arrears?*, above). More recent arrears may also be remitted for good cause, for example when the defaulter has been genuinely unemployed and unable to pay, and there is no real propspect of catching up.

METHODS OF ENFORCEMENT

Distress warrant
Distress (i.e. the seizure and sale of the defaulter's goods) is an essential consideration, even if not deployed often in practice. It can be useful where a defaulter is known to have significant assets—but for many people on low incomes the high level of costs involved and the often poor level of funds raised at auction simply serves to compound existing problems in trying to meet the order.

Postponement of distress
Where distress is used, the court can postpone the issue of a distress warrant on such terms as it sees fit. However, once a distress warrant has been issued, the court cannot suspend its operation. So in one case where the bailiff took 'walking possession of the defaulter's goods and chattels', it was too late for the defaulter to request suspension. It is not necessary for there to be proof of any 'wilful refusal or culpable neglect' for the justices to consider distress. There is also no time limit to the levying of distress once the warrant is issued.

Attachment of earnings (AEO)
Where there is steady employment, an attachment of earnings order (AEO) is often appropriate. This is an instruction to the employer of the defaulter to make deductions from the latter's earnings and send these to the collecting officer. Where the debtor frequently changes employment an AEO is not usually appropriate.

Earnings include salary or wages, pensions and sick pay. They do not, however, include pay as a member of Her Majesty's forces. Service people are encouraged by their service units to make their own arrangements to pay maintenance orders. If default *does* occur, an application can be made to the service authorities for them to make deductions from pay. This, however, differs from a formal AEO as described in this section.

Application by the debtor
The debtor can apply for an AEO immediately on the making of the maintenance order—and many courts encourage such applications. Where the debtor does not apply, there must be a failure to make one or more payments under the order.

NDR and PER
The court has power to request a statement of earnings from the employer who will be asked to give particulars of the defaulter's earnings at present and as anticipated. The employer's written response is deemed to be evidence of its contents unless there is contrary proof. In making an AEO, the court must fix two rates:

- the normal deduction rate (NDR). This is a sum to be deducted from the debtor's earnings after allowance for income tax etc. It will be the amount of the order plus an amount in respect of the arrears. If earnings on any payment date are insufficient to cover the full NDR, the shortfall is made up from any surplus arising in later payment periods
- the protected earnings rate (PER). This is the level below which the defaulter's take home pay is not allowed to fall during each payment period. Where the PER is not reached, all the salary or wages due must be given to the defaulter. The PER reflects his or her needs and those of other people for whom he or she must reasonably provide. Thus, the court may, in appropriate cases, allow for the fact the defaulter has remarried and is supporting a second family. The PER ensures that the defaulter is left with sufficient income for necessities. It may be varied for up to four weeks by a single magistrate. Current state benefit rates merit consideration in assisting calculation of the PER.

An AEO does not cease when the arrears are paid. It continues to secure collection under the original order as payments fall due. However, the NDR will then be too high, so the collecting officer will apply for a downwards variation (to the level of the underlying periodic payment).

Other considerations
The employer can make a small deduction for each transaction to cover expenses. An offence is committed by the employer if he or she fails to comply with the order. A court is bound to make an AEO if appropriate rather than a commit someone to prison. An AEO ends if the defaulter is subsequently committed to prison for the arrears. Where there is loss or change of employment, the debtor must notify the court in writing— something which relates to any occasion when he or she leaves employment whilst the order is in force. The AEO will lapse until redirected to a new employer (or discharged). Once the court knows who a new employer is, it can redirect it without an application.

Imprisonment
Increasingly, courts have been required to justify any decisions to imprison for non-payment of money.

Last resort
Imprisonment (whether immediate or suspended) is the sanction of last resort—one which, in the case of a debt, is to be used sparingly.

Wilful refusal or culpable neglect
Following an inquiry into the defaulter's financial circumstances, there must be a finding of wilful refusal or culpable neglect. In effect, there must be deliberate defiance of the order or reckless disregard of it. Default through poverty or dilatoriness is not enough. Magistrates must consider the ability of the defaulter to make payments as at the date of the enforcement hearing. They cannot commit him or her to prison unless satisfied that *all other methods* have been considered—and if appropriate tried (or that they are likely to prove unsuccessful).

Young defaulters
Defaulters *under 17 years of age* cannot be sent to custody. In respect of people *under 21*, reasons must be stated in open court, and entered in the warrant and court register.

Presence of defendant
In respect of all imprisonment, it is necessary for the defaulter to be present at the hearing to which the means inquiry relates.

Legal advice

Any reasonable request for an adjournment to obtain legal advice should be allowed. The duty solicitor is available where someone is at risk of imprisonment.

Length of imprisonment in default

The maximum period for which someone can be sent to prison is determined by the amount of arrears to which the enforcement proceedings relate. The overall maximum is six weeks for an amount over £1000 (May, 1997). The statutory periods are as follows:

Arrears	Maximum imprisonment
not exceeding £200	7 days
exceeding £200 but not £500	14 days
exceeding £500 but not £1000	28 days
over £1000	six weeks

Effect of any payments on the term to be served

On payment in full, the committal lapses and, if already in custody, the defaulter is discharged. Serving part of the default period reduces the amount needed to secure release—broadly speaking, in proportion (seek legal advice).

Effect of imprisonment on arrears

Once a period of imprisonment in default has been served, the arrears are not wiped out but the defaulter cannot be imprisoned again for the self-same arrears (as opposed to new arrears). Other methods of enforcement can still be considered, such as distress or an AEO (above). However, this is frequently not productive and the collecting officer may well be compelled to mark the arrears in question 'unenforceable'—and ultimately to apply to the court for formal remission.

Suspended committal

Imprisonment in default can be suspended for a fixed time (for the defaulter to pay all the arrears) or on payment of amounts at regular intervals. In effect, the defaulter will need to pay amounts under the order as they fall due and reduce the arrears if he or she is to 'stay ahead'. However, in calculating whether a committal warrant should be issued, all amounts paid should first be appropriated to the arrears in respect of which the committal order was made. So, if the defaulter is supposed to pay an order of £10 per week and is £60 in arrears—and is then made the subject of a suspended committal on payment of £12 per week—(the order plus £2 per week off the arrears)—once he or she has cleared the £60, he or she is entitled to have the 'arrears' treated as paid. New enforcement proceedings will then be needed in respect of the fresh arrears which have accrued in the meantime. If a suspended committal is not complied with, the defaulter is sent a notice by the collecting officer. This invites written representations within eight days as to why the suspended committal should not be 'activated'. If the defaulter submits reasons (such as illness preventing earnings) these are placed before a single magistrate who can direct that the committal warrant to be released or that the matter be considered by a court. The single magistrate is likely to refer the matter to a court where there is, on the face of things, a change in circumstances. Where it *is* referred to a court, then notice must be given to the defaulter and the payee of the place and time of the hearing—but the court *can* proceed in the absence of either party. It may decide to:

- issue the warrant
- further postpone it until such time and on such terms as it thinks appropriate
- remit all or part of the arrears (part remission will reduce the period of imprisonment)
- not issue the warrant—if it thinks this appropriate and there has been a change of circumstances.

Review whilst in prison

When a defaulter is in prison, whether as a result of an immediate committal or the implementation of a suspended committal, he or she may apply for the matter to be reviewed. In the first instance, such an application is considered by a single magistrate. The magistrate will decide whether to refuse the application or place it before a court. If the matter *is* placed before a court, notice is given to the defaulter, the payee and the governor of the prison. However, even in the absence of any of these people at the hearing, the court can still deal with the application. It has various options, including remitting all or part of the arrears, directing that the warrant cease to have effect, further suspension on the same or new terms, or directing that the committal continue in effect.

ENFORCEMENT BY THE CSA

Assessment and collection of child maintenance by the Child Support Agency is discussed in *Chapter 5*. So far as enforcement is concerned, there are a number of powers available to the CSA. One of these—a 'deduction from earnings order'—does not, apart from a limited right of appeal, involve the courts. It is an administrative procedure. It is often used at the start of the enforcement process, but can be deployed when other methods have failed.

Liability orders
The CSA can apply to a magistrates' court for a liability order providing certain preconditions are satisfied, i.e. that:

- the liable person has failed to make one or more payments of child maintenance; and
  —a deduction of earnings order appears inappropriate (such as where the liable person is unemployed); or
  —a deduction of earnings order has been made, but has proved ineffective.

The liable person must be given seven days notice of the application. The court *cannot* question the original CSA assessment and must issue the liability order unless there is some procedural irregularity. In essence, the court is asked to confirm the debt. It will accordingly issue the liability order if satisfied that payments are due and have not been made.

A liability order authorises enforcement action to recover the debt. Most such action by the CSA does not involve the magistrates' court. It includes distress (when bailiffs are instructed to seize and sell the defaulter's goods)—and if this is unsuccessful application can be made in the county court for a charging order or garnishee order. The former involves a charge on property so that, if sold, the proceeds of sale are released to the CSA up to the amount of the liability order. A garnishee order involves accessing a bank account and requiring the release of funds held in it.

Committal to prison
The CSA can apply to the family proceedings court for the defaulter to be committed to prison—but only where other forms of enforcement have failed. Analogous principles to those stated earlier in this chapter then come into play. The maximum period of imprisonment is six weeks and there must be a finding of wilful refusal or culpable neglect. Imprisonment can be immediate or suspended and the debtor must be present. A part payment reduces any imprisonment ordered in proportion—and the same notice and review procedures apply as for those other court orders involving imprisonment in default already described above.

CHAPTER 7

Domestic Violence and Occupation Orders

The Law Commission report *Domestic Violence and Occupation of the Family Home* (1992) addressed two 'distinct but inseparable problems':

- protection within the family from molestation or violence; and
- occupation of the family home when relationships break down, either temporarily or permanently.

The existing law in this field was described as complex, confusing and lacking in integration. The Law Commission made several proposals which, after revision, found their way into the Family Law Act 1996. To understand the operation of Part IV of the 1996 Act (in which the relevant provisions are contained) an outline of the Act's overall structure is instructive.

THE FAMILY LAW ACT 1996

The 1996 Act deals with various aspects of family proceedings:

- *Part I* contains the *underlying principles* affecting Parts II and III
- *Part II* deals with divorce and separation. These provisions are not expected to come into force until 1999 at the earliest, but certain parts of the country may become pilot areas for certain provisions relating to information sessions, etc. (see later in this chapter)
- *Part III* concerns legal aid and mediation. It has relevance to the operation of Part IV, below. It came into force on 1 April 1997
- *Part IV* is expected to come into force on 1 October 1997. It directly concerns the family proceedings court and deals with:
    —domestic violence; and
    —occupation of the family home
- *Part V* contains supplemental provisions. One of particular relevance to the family proceedings court is the power to make regulations to provide for the separate representation of children in certain proceedings (which could include Part IV proceedings).

Some preliminary understanding of Parts I, II and III of the Act is required before Part IV can be fully appreciated. Only Part II and certain schedules to the Act have no direct application to family proceedings court. Parts I to III are best understood in reverse order.

Part III Legal aid and mediation

Part III of the Act seeks to divert legal aid funds away from costly—often bitter and protracted—litigation towards helping parties to reach a negotiated, agreed and hopefully firmer and more acceptable outcome. The provision of public funds will be considered (subject to means testing) towards the use of mediation facilities in 'disputes relating to family matters'. Such 'family matters' include proceedings affected by:

- existing divorce law (in the Matrimonial Causes Act 1973)
- the new divorce law (in Part II of the 1996 Act)
- the new provisions about domestic violence and occupation of the family home (in Part IV of the 1996 Act)
- the Children Act 1989 (including, for example, section 8 orders in care proceedings: *Chapter 2).*

The Act allows the Legal Aid Board to 'secure mediation' before considering the grant of legal aid for court proceedings. In some cases therefore, parties will not get legal aid unless mediation has first been attempted. Legal aid is means tested. People paying for their own lawyer, or not wishing to be represented by one, will, if they choose, be able to move directly to court proceedings (equally, of course, such people will not receive financial assistance if mediation facilities *are* desired. However, the Lord Chancellor can make grants in connection with the general provision of 'marriage support services').

A code of practice will apply to mediators operating pursuant to Part III. It is likely that Part III mediation will be franchised to various bodies (including firms of solicitors or barristers' chambers, as well as to existing mediation bodies) and there is likely to be growth in this field.

Although the new law will enable the Legal Aid Board to offer free or subsidised mediation before considering legal aid, the Board will not be able to insist on this alternative approach in cases under Part IV of the 1996 Act ('domestic violence' and occupation of the family home) or under Parts IV and V of the Children Act 1989 (e.g. applications for care or supervision orders, or emergency protection orders: *Chapter 2*).

Part II Divorce and separation

The law concerning divorce and separation will be totally revised and, in particular, Part II will provide for *no fault* divorce, abolish the decree nisi and the decree absolute, and radically alter procedures. Although family proceedings courts do not deal with divorce (*Chapter 1*), certain aspects of the changes are worth noting for their 'knock on' potential. First, in most cases the parties to the case, before starting out on divorce proceedings, will need to attend an 'information meeting' which will cover issues such as:

- what facilities exist to help parties save their marriage (counselling aimed at reconciliation)
- what the new divorce procedure involves
- what facilities exist to help the parties negotiate rather than litigate their divorce if it is to proceed.

The government has initiated pilot projects to test how information meetings work in practice. When the new divorce law is implemented, the existence generally of such meetings will be of relevance to proceedings in family proceedings courts. Information given at a meeting may be relevant for parties engaged in litigation before magistrates, and magistrates may be able to refer parties to such meetings in appropriate circumstances.

Second, as a result of the new law, in practice no marriage can end in divorce until at least two years from the date of the marriage. This may mean more proceedings being taken by parties in the family proceedings court ahead of divorce proceedings than previously.

Part I: General Principles for Part II (Divorce, Separation and Marriage Counselling) and Part III (Legal Aid and Mediation)
Part I of the 1996 Act requires the court and other people operating under Parts II and III to observe certain fundamental principles. Whilst not directly relevant to family proceedings courts dealing with Part IV non-molestation or occupation applications, future relevant case law is likely to reflect these principles. They can be summarised:

- *The institution of marriage should be supported* It is unclear what this principle (which was also a general theme within the conservative government responsible for the 1996 Act) will add beyond the general reconciliation provisions
- *Spouses should be encouraged to save their marriage* As already intimated in relation to Part III (mediation) above, reconciliation is to be encouraged—and spouses to take all practical steps to save their marriage, and to seek help through counselling or other avenues. Public money is scheduled to be put into counselling and marriage support services

- *Breakdown of marriage* On the irretrievable breakdown of a marriage, courts and all people involved should aim for minimum distress, good and continuing relationships and the avoidance of unreasonable costs
- *Domestic violence* The court and all concerned must work towards removing or diminishing the risk of violence.

Terminology

In connection with the family support service being introduced by the 1996 Act, three aspects need to be distinguished:

- *information meetings* which will take place prior to divorce
- *counselling* i.e. assistance towards reconciliation; and
- *mediation* i.e. assistance in negotiating outcomes to family disputes rather than resort to litigation.

Family panel members and other practitioners need to be precise in their use of this terminology, and to be familiar with services in their own area.

CHANGES TO THE CHILDREN ACT 1989

The Family Law Act 1996 alters the Children Act 1989 and gives additional powers to courts dealing with applications for interim care orders or emergency protection orders (likely effective date 1 October 1997). Emergency protection orders can only be made by the family proceedings court, and all care proceedings are commenced there.

Exclusion requirements

The changes seek to address the problem (which often occurs) where alleged sexual or physical abuse has taken place and it appears that it would not be safe for the child to remain in the environment where the alleged abuser lives. Under existing law, the child may have to be removed from that environment—and thus face disruption—whilst the alleged perpetrator continues to live in the home.

The changes allow courts to consider making an 'exclusion requirement' requiring the alleged abuser to leave the home providing there is someone else living in the same dwelling house as the child who is able and willing to give the child the care a reasonable parent would, and that person consents to the exclusion requirement. Comparable exclusion provisions are enacted concerning emergency protection orders. (These effects are achieved by new sections of the Children Act 1989: 38A and 38B (interim care) and 44A and 44B (emergency protection)). Experience will show the extent to which exclusion interacts with non-molestation and occupation orders (below), or prohibited steps orders (*Chapter 2*) to provide a 'menu' of family protection measures.

Welfare of the child

Some legal subtleties are likely to occur when courts are asked to compare aspects of Part IV of the 1996 Act with provisions of the Children Act 1989. When dealing with an application for a non-molestation order or an occupation order, the court must consider the interests of a 'relevant child', defined as:

- a child who is living with or who might reasonably be expected to live with either party to the proceedings
- any child in the proceedings in respect of whom an order under the Children Act 1989 (*Chapter 2*) or Adoption Act 1976 (*Chapter 8*) is in question; or
- any other child whose interests the court considers relevant.

This is a wide definition. As emphasised in *Chapter 4* of this handbook, the Children Act 1989 requires that a court's paramount consideration *shall be* the child's welfare whenever it is considering the child's upbringing. The 1989 Act also provides a 'welfare checklist' which must be considered by the court in, for example, care proceedings or whenever there is a contested section 8 application. Part IV of the 1996 Act does not incorporate these principles, but concepts such as the health, safety and well being of the relevant child.

It will be seen later in this chapter when dealing with occupation orders that there is, in relation to applications for those orders, a 'balance of harm' test, which—put simply—may in some circumstances present the court virtually with a duty to make an occupation order. The balance of harm test can also sometimes apply if the court thinks there is a risk of 'significant harm' to a relevant child. It is not entirely clear if this variety of significant harm is identical to that affecting the threshold criteria for care orders (*Chapter 2*). Differences of terminology when dealing with child welfare are of concern. It will take case law to show exactly how certain matters are to be reconciled.

'DOMESTIC VIOLENCE': NON-MOLESTATION ORDERS

Section 42 of the 1996 Act deals with the power to make non-molestation orders (likely effective date 1 October 1997). The Lord Chancellor has power to specify that certain types of proceedings will commence in a given level of court. At the time of writing (May, 1997), the indications are that in respect of non-molestation applications (and occupation applications: next section) an applicant will have *a choice* whether to start in the family proceedings court, the county court or High Court. However, it is likely that the Legal Aid Board will attach a condition to most legal aid certificates requiring the non-molestation proceedings to be commenced in the family proceedings court.

What is a non-molestation order?
A non-molestation order prohibits the respondent from molesting a named individual who is 'associated' with him or her or from molesting a relevant child. The meaning of 'associated person' is dealt with later in this section.

Molestation
Prior to Part IV of the 1996 Act, family proceedings courts had limited powers under the Domestic Proceedings and Magistrates' Courts Act 1978 to make orders protecting victims of domestic violence, but only in circumstances where there was the use or threat of violence—and orders only prohibited these forms of behaviour. The county court and the High Court could make orders concerning molestation (a far wider concept) under the Domestic Violence and Matrimonial Proceedings Act 1976.

There is no statutory definition of 'molestation'. One dictionary definition is 'to disturb or annoy by benevolent interference or to accost or attack'. A quotation from the Law Commission Report *Family Law, Domestic Violence and Occupation of Family Home* (1994) may assist:

> Molestation is an umbrella term which covers a wide range of behaviour. It includes any form of serious pestering or harassment . . . Any conduct which could properly be regarded as such a degree of harassment as to call for the intervention of the court . . . The degree of severity depends less upon its intrinsic nature than upon it being part of a pattern and upon its effect on the victim.

There is a good deal of case law on the meaning of molestation under the jurisdiction that the county court and High Court exercised prior to the 1996 Act. However, the statutory provisions governing their jurisdiction are repealed when Part IV of the 1996 Act comes into force. It thus remains to be seen how the former case law on molestation will be applied, particularly as the remedy can now be considered for a greater range of people than before: seek legal advice concerning the current position.

Criteria for a non-molestation order

The court must have regard 'to all the circumstances' including the need to secure the health, safety and well being of:

- the applicant; or
- the person for whose benefit the order will be made; and
- any relevant child.

Duration of orders

A non-molestation order can be for a fixed period or until further order—but if made in other family proceedings (i.e. not proceedings exclusively to deal with non-molestation) the order will cease if that application is withdrawn or dismissed. The practice of the county court has been to regard non-molestation orders as *temporary* measures.

Who can apply?

Whenever it is dealing with any 'family proceedings' (see *Part Two* of this handbook for the full definition) the court can make a non-molestation order *of its own motion*. If, for example, an application is made under section 8 Children Act 1989 it is open to the court, if it thinks it is necessary, to make such an order, even though nobody has applied for one. The following people *can* apply for a non-molestation order:

- associated persons (below)
- authorised third parties (if these come into being: below); or
- children under sixteen years of age (who need the leave of the court. The government stated that its intention was that their applications should be made to the High Court).

The Lord Chancellor is empowered to authorise third parties to bring proceedings on behalf of an 'associated person'. An obvious potential 'third party' would be the police. Parliament considered that some victims were fearful of court proceedings, and it might serve their interests if the police made the application. Traditionally police forces have been reluctant to become embroiled in *civil matters* (i.e. essentially private disputes between individuals)—so that it remains to be seen what practices emerge. *Criminal* proceedings are not barred, of course, where violence or criminal threats are involved, especially where the matter is of such seriousness that events cannot be disregarded.

105

Meaning of 'associated person'

The great majority of applications for non-molestation orders are likely to be by associated persons. Prior to the Act, only spouses could apply, and in the county court and High Court 'cohabitants' in addition. The new definition of associated person is far wider—and is also relevant when considering applications for certain categories of occupation order (below). It includes people who:

- are or have been married to each other
- are cohabitants or former cohabitants (further details concerning cohabitants can be found in the section of this chapter dealing with *Occupation Orders*)
- live, or have lived, in the same household other than by reason of one of them being the other's employee, a tenant, lodger or boarder. An example might be students or other people who share a house or flat rented to them by a third party
- are relatives. The statutory list of relatives is wide-ranging and includes: father, mother, step-father, step-mother, son, daughter, step-son, step-daughter, grandmother, grandfather, grandson, brother, sister, uncle, aunt, niece, nephew
- have agreed to marry one another. Proof of whether or not people are engaged to be married can be provided in various ways set out in the Act. Where an agreement to marry is terminated, no application can be made for a non-molestation order after three years from the date of that termination. This bar is also applicable to applications for occupation orders
- in relation to a relevant child, are either a parent or have parental responsibility
- in relation to a relevant child who has been freed for adoption, are the natural or adoptive parents of the adopted child, the natural grandparents of the adopted child, or any person with whom the child has at any time been placed for adoption; and
- parties to existing family proceedings (other than those involving domestic violence or other applications under Part IV of the 1989 Act).

Variation and discharge

A non-molestation order can be varied or discharged by the court on application by the respondent or the person who originally applied for it. If the court made the order of its own motion, the court itself can also discharge or vary it, in this case without an application.

Content of the order

The court may make an order prohibiting specific types of molestation or molestation generally. However, the order must be sufficiently defined to make sure that:

- the respondent can know what acts, etc. are prohibited; and
- enforcement is straightforward.

Ex parte applications

In relation to both non-molestation orders and occupation orders (below), notice must normally be given to the other party or parties and the hearing takes place with all concerned present. In exceptional circumstances, an *ex parte* application can be made, i.e. where the court hears only from one party, the individual applying for the order. The court must have regard to all the circumstances, including any risk of significant harm to the applicant or relevant child if the order is not made immediately, and whether or not it is likely that the applicant will be deterred or prevented from pursuing the application if an order is not made forthwith.

The court can also make an *ex parte* order when there is reason to believe that the respondent is aware of the proceedings but is deliberately evading service.

If an *ex parte* order is granted the court must allow representations as soon as this is just and convenient.

Appeal

Appeals against decisions of the family proceeding court in relation to a non-molestation orders are made to the High Court.

Protection from Harassment Act 1997

Although not directly relevant to this handbook, the remedies provided by this Act will need to be considered by magistrates and practitioners in the ordinary magistrates' court. The remedies provided by the 1997 Act in some cases overlap with the non-molestation provisions described above. The majority of the Protection from Harassment Act came into force in June, 1997: seek legal advice.

OCCUPATION ORDERS

When the relevant provisions of the Family Law Act 1996 are in force (likely effective date 1 October 1997). Courts are given power to regulate the occupation of 'the family home'. Magistrates on the family panel will share this jurisdiction with the High Court and county court in most instances. At the time of writing, it seems likely that the majority of such applications will be dealt with by the county court, but it remains necessary for family panel members and other practitioners to be familiar with the legal provisions in readiness for those cases which do filter into the family proceedings court.

FIVE CATEGORIES OF ORDER

In practice, orders are described by reference to 'Categories 1 to 5' below. It is essential to know which category an applicant falls into since this will affect:

- the criteria which the court must consider when deciding whether to grant the application
- the content of the order; and
- the duration of the order.

If an applicant applies under the wrong category, the court can determine to treat the application as if made within the right category.

Category 1 : Where the applicant is entitled to occupy the property
Where the applicant is entitled to occupy the home, either by virtue of the general law or 'matrimonial home rights', he or she may apply for an order against anyone with whom the applicant is 'associated' (as defined under *Non-molestation Orders*, above) provided that the home is or was intended to be their common home.

What are matrimonial home rights?
The law has for some time allowed a spouse who has no property rights in connection with the family home to be protected from eviction, or if he or she has been unlawfully evicted, to apply for leave to reoccupy the house. These rights are known as 'matrimonial home rights'. Any one with such rights is entitled to apply under this category—as well as a spouse who has a right to occupy by virtue of, say a legal tenancy or joint ownership.

What type of order can be made?
Two types of orders can be made in respect of *Category 1* applicants:

- *a declaratory order* This simply declares that the applicant has matrimonial home rights in a house in respect of which there may be a dispute, for example as to whether the house is in fact a family home or, say, a house used for investment purposes. Matrimonial home rights normally cease on divorce (or death). Under this category, an application can be made for the rights to be extended. A spouse could apply for his or her right not to be evicted without the leave the court to be extended beyond divorce. The court has a wide discretion, i.e. to 'exercise its powers . . . in any case where it considers that in all the circumstances it is just and reasonable.' The power to make a declaratory order is by its very nature only applicable to spouses.
- *a regulatory order* This power exists where either party is 'associated' with the other (see under *Non-molestation Orders*) and therefore could include, for example, a brother and sister living in the same house if it was their joint family home. A regulatory order can contain a provision such as a requirement for one of the parties to leave the house, or it could affect the actual occupation of the house (e.g. a requirement for one party to live in one part of it and the other party in another). In deciding whether a regulatory order is appropriate the court must have regard to all the circumstances and in particular:
    - —the housing needs and resources of the parties and any children
    - —the financial resources of the parties
    - —the likely effect of an order (or lack of one) on the health, safety and well being of the parties or any relevant child; and
    - —the conduct of the parties in relation to each other and otherwise.

Balance of harm

The above factors are also subject to a 'balance of harm' test: an important new concept. The test, states:

> If it appears to the court that the applicant or any relevant child is likely to suffer significant harm attributable to conduct of the respondent if an order under this section containing one or more of the provisions mentioned in sub-section (3) is not made, the court shall make the order unless it appears to it that—

(a) the respondent or any relevant child is likely to suffer significant harm if the order is made; and

(b) the harm likely to be suffered by the respondent or child in that event is as great as, or greater than, the harm attributable to the conduct of the respondent which is likely to be suffered by the applicant or child if the order is not made. (Section 33(7) Family Law Act 1996)

The reasoning behind the test and the effect it will have in practice was predicted by the Law Commission in the report mentioned at the beginning of this chapter:

> In cases where the question of significant harm does not arise, the court would have power to make an order taking into account . . . (relevant) factors . . . but, in cases where there is a likelihood of significant harm this power becomes a duty and the court must make the order after balancing the degree of harm likely to be suffered by both parties and any children concerned. This approach would still work in cases of cross application where the court would firstly consider who would suffer the greatest risk of harm if the order were not made. In the event of the balance of harm being equal, the court would retain power to make an order, but would have no duty to do so, and would still be able to reach the right result. Harm has a narrower meaning than hardship. It is defined as 'ill-treatment or impairment of physical or mental health.' In relation to children the term will attract the definition used in section 31 Children Act 1989. It is likely that a respondent threatened with ouster on account of his violence would be able to establish a degree of hardship, but he is unlikely to suffer significant harm whereas his wife and children who are being subject to his violence or abuse may very easily suffer harm if he remains in the house. In this way the court will be treating violence or other forms of abuse as deserving immediate relief, and will be directed to make an order where significant harm exists.

How long can a Category 1 regulatory order last?

Declaratory orders are not affected by time considerations. A *regulatory* order may—with continuing effect—be for a fixed period, until the occurrence of a specified event, or 'until further order.' It cannot be for an indeterminate period. The former 'ouster' order in the county court (the nearest comparable order) was treated as a *temporary* measure, to give time for parties to resolve their dispute permanently. The law on occupation orders is likely to develop in the same way.

Category 2: Where the applicant is a former spouse with no existing right to occupy and the respondent the other former spouse with a legal right to occupy

When a spouse has matrimonial home rights he or she can apply under *Category 1*. On divorce, such rights come to an end unless extended by a court following an application under *Category 1*. Where this has not happened, a former spouse can apply for an order under *Category 2*.

What type of order can be obtained?

If a court decides to grant an occupation order under this category it must contain a *declaratory* provision giving similar rights to the former spouse that he or she would have had if the marriage had not come to an end and the spouse had matrimonial home rights. In other words, if the court considers that an order should be made, the applicant who is the former spouse should, at the very least, be put into the same position as if the marriage had continued. In addition, the court has a discretion to make provision *regulating* occupation of the property similar to those described in relation to *Category 1* (e.g. requiring the respondent to leave or excluding him or her from a defined area of the premises).

Criteria

In deciding whether to grant an occupation order, the court will consider similar factors to those mentioned in relation to *Category 1*. In addition, three factors specific to ex-spouses not entitled to occupy the property must be considered. These are:

- the length of time since the parties ceased to live together
- the length of time since the marriage was dissolved or annulled; and
- the existence of certain pending proceedings between the parties.

In some circumstances it will be *more* difficult to obtain an occupation order. If a significant time has elapsed between the parties ceasing to live together or the marriage ending, this would tend to tell against making an order. If other proceedings are pending in connection with the former matrimonial home, the family proceedings court may well consider that an occupation order would not be appropriate. The other court would in most cases be able to deal with such outstanding matters.

Balance of harm

The balance of harm test described under *Category 1* applies.

How long can a Category 2 order last for?
One difference between *Category 1* and *Category 2* is that the latter type of order cannot continue after the death of either party, and must be for a maximum of six months—although this can be renewed.

Category 3: Where the applicant is a 'cohabitant' or 'ex-cohabitant' without an existing right to occupy

In such circumstances the other party will be the corresponding cohabitant or ex-cohabitant who has a right to occupy.

Definition of 'cohabitant'
The Act defines cohabitants as follows:

(a) 'cohabitants' are a man and a woman who, although not married to each other, are living together as husband and wife; and
(b) 'former cohabitants' is to be read accordingly, but does not include cohabitants who have subsequently married each other.
(Section 62(1))

Couples must have lived together as 'husband and wife' (so that gay couples are seemingly excluded as the law stands). This will normally involve a shared life and living arrangements and a sexual element. Existing case law will probably be applicable to disputes about whether someone is a cohabitant: seek legal advice.

What can the order contain?
As with *Category 2*, when an order is made certain *declaratory* provisions must be inserted which are similar to those a spouse would obtain who had matrimonial home rights. In addition, the court has a discretion to impose *regulatory* provisions similar to those under *Category 1*.

Criteria
Similar factors must be considered under *Category 3* as in the previous two categories. In addition, the court must take into account certain factors specific to cohabitants. These are:

- the nature of the parties' relationship
- whether there are or have been any children who are children of both parties of whom both parties have or have had parental responsibility; and
- the length of time during which they have lived together as husband and wife.

112

Although the court must consider the likelihood of a party or any child suffering significant harm attributable to contact with the respondent, these questions do *not* impose a duty on the court to make the order: contrast the position in relation to spouses and entitled parties.

How long can the order last?
A *Category 3* order may be made only for a maximum period of six months and may be renewed only once.

Category 4: Where the applicant is a spouse or ex-spouse and neither the applicant or the respondent has a right to occupy

A spouse or ex-spouse may make an application for an order where neither party is entitled to occupy the property. In this case the order will only operate as between the parties and not affect a third party (who may, e.g. be entitled to occupy the property). An example of such a situation could be where parties have married but not got a home of their own, and are, say, living with in-laws.

What can the order contain?
The order will only contain *regulatory* provisions, similar to those described in relation to *Category 1*. It is not appropriate under this heading for there to be any *declaratory* provisions as none of the parties have rights of occupation of the home.

Criteria
Category 4 has a list of factors similar to those in relation to *Category 1*. The one main difference between an applicant under *Category 4* and one under *Category 1* is that both parties must be in occupation.

Balance of harm
The balance of harm test applies.

How long can the order last for?
An order under *Category 4* may be for a maximum period of six months, but can be renewed.

Category 5: Where the applicant is a cohabitant or ex-cohabitant and neither the applicant nor the respondent has a right to occupy

A cohabitant or ex-cohabitant may make an application for an order where neither party is entitled to occupy the property. In this case the order will only operate as between the parties and not, for example, affect a third party entitled to occupy the property.

What can the order contain?
The position is identical to that in relation to *Category 4*.

Criteria
The following basic items need to be considered:

- the financial needs of the parties
- the financial resources of the parties
- the effect of any order or lack of one on the health, safety and well being of the parties or any relevant child; and
- the conduct of the parties.

However, the law is particularly complex regarding the criteria for *Category 5* applications and legal advice should be sought. The test relating to 'significant harm' operates in the same way as it does in relation to a non-entitled cohabitant against an entitled cohabitant under *Category 3*. It does not impose a duty on the court to make an order.

How long can the order last for?
A *Category 5* order can be for a maximum of six months and is renewable, but only once.

Other matters affecting occupation
Several general items are relevant when considering the above applications. These are as follows:

- *marriage and commitment* It might be thought that all people, whatever their status, should be treated in the same way by courts. However, due to pressure in Parliament an amendment was agreed to the 1996 Act by the government (now contained in section 41). The provision states that when dealing with an application by a cohabitant or ex-cohabitant the court '. . . is to have regard to the fact that they have not given each other the commitment involved in marriage.'
- *ancillary orders* When a court makes an order against an entitled respondent it may make an ancillary order imposing certain obligations on either party, or granting either possession or use of furniture or other home contents. Such obligations may relate to:
  —repair and maintenance of the home
  —discharge of outgoings (e.g. rent, mortgage)
  —payment of rent to the party who has been ousted
  —taking reasonable care of the furniture or other contents; or
  —taking reasonable steps to keep the home and contents secure.

- *child applicants* A child under 16 years of age may apply for an occupation order but only with the leave of the court. Leave will only be granted if the court is satisfied that the child has sufficient understanding. It is likely that rules will stipulate that such applications must be made to the High Court.
- *power to make an order of the court's own motion* Whereas in any family proceedings a court can make a *non-molestation order* of its own motion, i.e. without an application from a party, no such inherent power extends to occupation orders. A court can only make an occupation order if someone applies for one.

Readers are referred to the notes dealing with *ex parte* orders, powers of arrest, enforcement and general matters which appear elsewhere in this chapter.

UNDERTAKINGS

Under pre-1996 Act procedures, the county court and High Court when dealing with applications for non-molestation orders accepted undertakings. This concept is new to the family proceedings court, but in certain circumstances undertakings will be possible under Part IV of the 1996 Act: see the specimen form in *Part Two* of this handbook.

An undertaking is a promise by a party to do or not to do some specified act, or, for example, to agree to do something, such as leave the home. An undertaking can function as an alternative to a non-molestation or occupation order if accepted by a party to such proceedings and, in one instance (below), approved by the court.

Under Part IV, an undertaking cannot be accepted in situations where the court, if making an order, would have attached a power of arrest. As will be seen in the notes on enforcement later in this chapter, if the applicant has alleged violence or threatened violence by the respondent against the applicant or a relevant child, then, if those allegations are proved, a power of arrest should be attached to the order.

If an undertaking is offered in situations where violence or threats of violence have actually occured, it cannot be accepted—but presumably where the application alleges violence, but then the parties, both legally represented, ask the court to accept an undertaking and specifically not to rule on the issue of violence, it is arguable that an undertaking might be acceptable.

Effect of an undertaking
If the parties agree an undertaking the court cannot refuse to accept it other than in the situation already mentioned above. Neither can the

court insist that the allegations are proved, and it cannot proceed to make an order.

An undertaking is often viewed as having advantages. From the respondent's point of view, it means that he or she does not have to admit the facts. From the court's point of view, it avoids the need for a contested hearing. From the applicant's point of view, he or she is given similar protection to when an order is made. The only difference— though perhaps important—is that a power of arrest can only be attached to a court order. However, if an undertaking is breached there is no reason why an application for an order, or emergency protection, should not follow.

The process of giving an undertaking

At the time of writing (May, 1997), the statutory rules detailing the way in which undertakings should be given in family proceedings courts have not been made. It is likely that there will be a similar procedure to that existing in the county court before the 1996 Act. If so, undertakings may be given to the court in writing on a prescribed form. It may be that the rules will be flexible enough to allow the respondent's legal representative to certify agreement, and that an explanation has been given to the respondent about the effect of the undertaking and his or her responsibilities and that he or she understands it. If so, it may also be necessary to produce written confirmation of such 'out of court' agreement signed by the respondent.

A draft prescribed form of undertaking appears in *Part Two* of this handbook.

Enforcement of undertakings

An undertaking binds the giver from the moment it is accepted by the court and is enforceable as if it were an order of the court. The usual provisions in respect of disobedience of orders of magistrates' courts apply: *Chapter 6*.

Variation of undertakings

It is likely that an undertaking will be limited to a specified period of time, but it is still open for an undertaking, whilst in force, to be varied by the making of a subsequent undertaking on fresh terms.

POWERS OF ARREST

From the victim's point of view the sanction of the respondent being arrested by the police if he or she breaches a court order is likely to be a most effective one. The power of arrest stems from a direction contained within an order. This enables a constable to arrest *without warrant* someone who he or she has reasonable cause to suspect is in breach of the order. When a respondent is arrested he or she must be brought before the court within 24 hours (excluding Christmas Day, Good Friday and Sundays).

A power of arrest *must* be attached to an occupation order or a non-molestation order where both parties have had notice of the hearing and it appears there has been *actual* or *threatened violence* against the applicant or a relevant child, unless the court is satisfied that the applicant or relevant child will be adequately protected without such a power. It is not easy to see circumstances where the court will be satisfied that the relevant people will be so protected without a power of arrest.

Where an order has been made on an *ex parte* basis the court is not under a mandatory duty to attach a power of arrest. Instead it has a *discretion* whether to do so if it appears that the respondent:

- has used or threatened violence against the applicant or relevant child; and
- the applicant or relevant child is at risk of significant harm from the respondent if a power of arrest is not attached to the order immediately.

Duration of power of arrest
The power of arrest will usually last as long as the order does—but if such a power is attached to an order made *ex parte*, the court may provide that the power have effect for a shorter period than other parts of the order.

Application for the arrest of the respondent
Where a power of arrest has *not* been attached to the order and the applicant alleges that the respondent has breached the order, he or she may apply on oath for the respondent to be arrested. The court may grant that application if it has reasonable grounds for believing the applicant and that the respondent has failed to comply with the order.

Power to adjourn and remand
Whenever a respondent is brought before a court after having been arrested the court may either deal with the case immediately or, if appropriate, remand him or her to appear before the court at an adjourned hearing. Any remand may be on custody or on bail. Bail may be unconditional or subject to whatever conditions the court considers appropriate to ensure that he or she does not interfere with witnesses or

otherwise obstruct the course of justice. The Bail Act 1976 does not apply to this *civil* bail situation: seek legal advice.

In appropriate circumstances, the remand may be used to enable a medical examination and report concerning the respondent's physical or mental condition: seek legal advice.

GENERAL ENFORCEMENT POWERS

The effectiveness of the court's powers under Part IV of the 1996 Act to deter future violence or molestation will be judged by the effectiveness of enforcement. Apart from powers of arrest (which are not 'enforcement' in the strict sense), an understanding of general enforcement powers is essential for both magistrates and other practitioners. These powers are outlined in *Chapter 6.*

JURISDICTION OF MAGISTRATES' COURTS

Family proceedings courts will—subject to statutory rules to be made at the time of writing (May, 1997)—be able to deal with applications for both non-molestation orders and occupation orders. There is one proviso. Section 59 of the 1996 Act states that a magistrates' court is *not competent* to entertain any application or make any order involving

> any disputed question as to a party's entitlement to occupy any property by virtue of beneficial estate or interest or contract or by virtue of any enactment giving him the right to remain in occupation unless it is unnecessary to determine the question in order to deal with the application or make the order.

CHAPTER 8

Adoption

The Adoption Act 1976 and Magistrates' Courts (Adoption) Rules 1984 set out the law and procedure for adoption applications in magistrates' courts. Some changes were made by the Children Act 1989. The relevant law is also under review at the time of writing (May, 1997)—but no substantial changes are expected before the turn of the century.

Adoption proceedings are 'family proceedings' within the meaning of the Children Act 1989. This means that the court need not make an adoption order, but the order which best meets the needs of the child.

WHAT IS ADOPTION?

The idea of adoption is to provide a child with a secure and stable replacement family. An adopted child becomes a full member of the adoptive family, as if the adopters were his or her own parents. The order severs the existing legal relationship between the child and his or her real parents parents (usually called 'natural' or 'birth' parents) and the adoptive parents acquire parental responsibility (see, generally, *Chapter 2*). The child is given a new birth certificate in which he or she is described as the child of the adopters. The order extinguishes parental responsibility held by *any* other person, and, for example, *any* existing orders under the Children Act 1989, maintenance agreement or similar liability (such as an assessment under the Child Support Act 1991).

FREEING FOR ADOPTION

'Freeing for adoption' was introduced by the Children Act 1975. It was thought that finding adopters—and the adoption process itself—might be easier if the child was free for that purpose and prospective adopters could be assured at an early stage that a particular child was 'available'. A freeing order removes parenthood and gives parental responsibility to an adoption agency (see under *Adoption Agencies,* later in this chapter). The concept was imported from North America. Research in England and Wales, prior to 1975, showed that the then consent process was slow and often painful. A freeing order thus benefits both the natural parents and adoptive parents.

Procedure

The agency applies to the court by lodging an application form and relevant documents, including the child's birth certificate. The court can only make a freeing order if the parents or guardians of the child agree—unconditionally—to an adoption order being made or the court is satisfied that this agreement should be dispensed with. The grounds on which consent can be dispensed with are set out under the heading *Parental Responsibility* later in this chapter. The agency can only apply for consent to be dispensed with if the child is in its care.

Respondents to a freeing application

The respondents to a freeing application are:

- every parent who has parental responsibility
- every guardian of the child
- any local authority or voluntary organization which has parental responsibility for the child or is looking after or caring for the child
- anyone liable by virtue of any agreement or order to contribute to the maintenance of the child
- any other person or body who is made a respondent by direction of the court. The child *cannot* be a respondent. Someone liable to contribute to the child's upkeep by virtue of an assessment of the Child Support Agency—*Chapter 5*—is not a respondent under the last head. However, the court can direct that they be made such.

The decision of the court

The court must be satisfied that a freeing order will promote the welfare of the child—and there is a general duty to promote the welfare of all children, say, within a family. Before declaring that a child is free for adoption, the court must check whether the parents wish to make a declaration themselves to the effect that they prefer not to be involved in future questions concerning the adoption of the child. This enables them to sever their links with the child, which may be a less difficult way for them to deal with matters.

If a parent decides *not* to make such a declaration, progress reports must be made to former parents. The parents can still decide at any later stage to make a declaration that they do not wish to be involved. Conversely, where such a declaration *has* been made, if at any time more than 12 months after the freeing order no adoption order has been made or the child has not been placed for adoption, a parent can apply to the court to revoke any freeing order and to be allowed to resume parental responsibility.

A problem with seeking revocation of a freeing order is that, if revoked, any previous Children Act orders do not revive (e.g. affecting residence or contact: *Chapter 2*). If the child was in care prior to the freeing order, that care order does not come back into force—and the choice facing the court is between making no order—thereby leaving the child in a free for adoption 'Nomansland'—and revoking the order thereby returning full parental responsibility to the natural parents. This was the situation in *Re G* (1996) 2 FLR 398 where the mother accepted that rehabilitation with her was not an option. Seemingly, the closest thing to a solution lies in agencies not applying for freeing orders—and courts not making them—until all concerned are as sure as they can be about the future arrangements.

APPLYING FOR AN ADOPTION ORDER

Anyone can apply for an adoption order provided they satisfy certain statutory requirements:

- if *two people* wish to apply they must be married. (Unmarried couples *can* apply for a joint residence order—*Chapter 2*—or one of them could apply for an adoption order, followed, where appropriate, by a joint application for a residence order)
- both applicants must be at least 21 years old unless one of them is a parent of the child—when that applicant must be 18 or over, and the other at least 21
- at least one of the applicants must be domiciled (seek legal advice) in the United Kingdom.

The child
If the adoption is a 'step-parent adoption', or the child has been placed by an adoption agency, or by the High Court, then the child must be at least 19 weeks old. At all times during the preceding 13 weeks he or she must have had his or her home with the applicant or applicants, or one of them. In all other cases the child must be at least 12 months old and throughout the last 12 months must have had his or her home with the applicants, or one of them.

Procedure
Where the applicants chose to proceed in the family proceedings court, application is made to the court for the area within which the child (or if no freeing order has been made his or her parent or guardian) is living. A prescribed form must be completed and documentary evidence must be attached, such as marriage and birth certificates. Medical reports are

needed on the applicants and child where neither applicant is a natural parent. The court will check that all procedural requirements are met, for example if the case is one where three months notification must be given to the local authority whether this has occurred.

Respondents
The respondents to an adoption application are:

- every parent or guardian—unless the child is free for adoption (above)
- any adoption agency
  - with parental responsibility
  - which has been named in the application form or in any form of agreement to the making of the adoption order as having taken part in the arrangements for the adoption of the child
- any local authority to whom the applicant has given notice of his or her intention to apply for an adoption order
- any local authority or voluntary organization which has parental responsibility for, is looking after, or is caring for the child
- where the applicant is applying on his or her own but is married and proposes to argue that he or she has separated from his or her spouse and that separation is likely to be permanent, the other spouse
- possibly an unmarried father—see below—or any other person or body that the court directs should be made a respondent. The child *cannot* be a respondent.

A hearing date is then fixed and notice served by the court on all parties, the reporting officer (below) and the guardian ad litem, if appointed (below). All people who have been given notice may attend the hearing and be heard on whether or not an adoption order should be made. The applicants and child *must* attend personally, although, as already stated, the child is not a party.

The position of unmarried fathers
The definition of 'parent' in the Adoption Act 1976 is narrower than that in the Children Act 1989—extending only to fathers who have parental responsibility. However, the Adoption Rules provide that someone is a respondent if liable under a maintenance order or agreement and the court has a general discretion to add respondents (above). Also, to ensure that a child is not freed without examining all options, one of the duties of a reporting officer is to interview any person claiming to be the

father of the child to assist the court in satisfying itself, before any freeing order or adoption order is made, that he:

- has no intention of applying for a parental responsibility order or a residence order (i.e. under the Children Act 1989: *Chapter 2*); or
- if he did make such an application, that it would be likely to be refused.

WELFARE OF THE CHILD

The 1976 Act makes clear that in reaching any decision relating to freeing for adoption or adoption, a court or adoption agency must have regard to all the circumstances, *first consideration* being given to the need to safeguard and promote the welfare of the child throughout his or her childhood. There is also a duty, as far as practicable, to ascertain the *wishes and feelings* of the child and give these due consideration. The long term future of the child thus has to be considered. Concerning how much weight should be attached to a child's welfare, the Lord Chancellor stated in 1975:

> to make the child's welfare *first consideration* is clearly intended to mean that the child's interest is to be weighted — but the question of weighted by how much is not answered.

Religious upbringing
An adoption agency must have regard, as far as is practicable, to any wishes of a child's parents or guardians in so far as religious upbringing is concerned.

PARENTAL CONSENT

An adoption order or freeing order (whichever is relevant) cannot be made unless each parent with parental responsibility freely and unconditionally agrees to the making of the order. Agreement cannot be given by a mother until her child is at least six weeks old—a safeguard intended to ensure that she has recovered from the effects of childbirth. However, the court has a general power to dispense with a parent's agreement where the parent:

- cannot be found or is incapable of giving agreement
- is withholding agreement unreasonably

- has persistently failed without reasonable cause to discharge his or her parental responsibility for the child
- has abandoned or neglected the child
- has persistently ill-treated the child; or
- has seriously ill-treated the child and rehabilitation is unlikely.

Various rulings have been given concerning the withholding of consent. In *Re L* (1962) 106 Sol Jo 611, Lord Denning, Master of the Rolls, suggested the following approach:

- the question whether consent is being unreasonably withheld is to be judged at the date of the hearing
- the welfare of the child is not the *sole* consideration
- the one question is whether the parent is unreasonably withholding consent
- in considering whether the parent is reasonable or unreasonable the court must take into account the welfare of the child
- a reasonable parent gives great weight to what is better for the child; and
- the court must look and see whether the parent is being unreasonable according to what a reasonable parent would do in the particular circumstances.

The court must also apply the welfare test—in effect decide whether the adoption or freeing order is in the child's best interests—*before* deciding whether to dispense with parental agreement. Where the applicant intends to ask the court to do this, the request must appear in the application, or a subsequent notice to the court—and three copies of the statement of facts on which he or she intends to rely must be provided.

GUARDIANS AD LITEM AND REPORTING OFFICERS

As explained in *Chapter 2*, every local authority must establish a Panel of Guardians ad Litem and Reporting Officers (GALROs). Where everyone appears to be in agreement about the adoption, a *reporting officer* is appointed. In other situations the court has a discretion to appoint a *guardian ad litem.*

Appointment of a guardian ad litem
As soon as possible after an adoption application or freeing application is made, the justices' clerk must appoint a guardian ad litem, when:

- the child is not free for adoption and it appears that a parent or guardian is unwilling to agree; or
- there are special circumstances and this appears necessary for the welfare of the child.

If agreement *is* forthcoming, a 'reporting officer' is appointed instead. It is possible for a parent who appears to be willing to agree to change his or her mind. In such a case the court would change the appointment from that of reporting officer to that of a guardian ad litem. It is therefore important that the two roles can be carried out by the same individual and that people appointed to the GALRO panel are qualified to act in either capacity.

Duties of the guardian

The guardian's duties are, with a view to safeguarding the interests of the child, to:

- investigate all relevant matters
- advise on the child's presence at the hearing
- perform such other duties as the court directs or as appear necessary
- write a report to the court, including an interim report if directed by the court to do so
- attend any hearing; and
- perform any other duties as directed by the court.

As already indicated, the child is *not* a party to the proceedings and therefore the guardian will not have the benefit of a solicitor for the child to work with him or her (as he or she will in *public law* proceedings: *Chapter 2*).

In gathering information, the guardian will keep in mind those provisions of the Adoption Act 1976 which require a court to safeguard and promote the welfare of the child, and, as far as practicable, ascertain the wishes and feelings of the child—and also deal with questions concerning religious upbringing, race, culture, and educational and emotional needs. He or she will need to inspect all documentary evidence and interview the child, the applicants, the parents and any other relevant people. The possibility of a section 8 order instead of adoption, or in addition, will need to be considered.

The guardian's report is confidential. This means that the parties are not entitled to see it or to be informed of its contents. Natural justice demands that if there are allegations in the report, the party concerned should have an opportunity to deal with these—and rules provide for the court to direct disclosure of all or part of the report.

In respect of the applicants and natural parents, consideration will need to be given to any counselling they have received and the question of contact, if any, after the adoption. In relation to the natural parents, question of consent, or withholding of agreement, will need to be discussed. Guardians may need to investigate a statement in support of dispensing with consent and the reasonableness or otherwise of a parent's refusal to agree to the adoption or freeing process.

In relation to freeing applications the guardian will consider the implications of the court making such an order. If there is no realistic chance of adoption the child could be left in 'limbo'.

If an order is made, the guardian should—if the child is of sufficient age and understanding—ensure that he or she comprehends the court's decision and its implications.

The reporting officer

Reporting officers were introduced by the Children Act 1975. Their basic task is to make sure that the natural parents fully understand the implications of their decision to consent and unconditionally give their agreement to the process. Statutory rules require that as soon as possible after the application for freeing or for adoption is made, the justices' clerk must appoint a reporting officer if the child is not free for adoption and it appears that a parent or guardian *is* willing to agree to an adoption order or freeing order. The reporting officer must also:

- witness the signature by the parent or guardian of the written agreement
- investigate all the circumstances relevant to that agreement
- write a report for the court
- obtain the directions of the court on any matter—in particular if a parent or guardian is unwilling to agree to the adoption or freeing
- perform such other duties as the court considers necessary; and
- attend any hearing if required.

In addition, in relation to freeing applications, the reporting officer has to:

- confirm that the parent or guardian has been given the opportunity of making a declaration that he or she prefers not to be involved in future questions concerning the adoption of the child; and

- to interview an unmarried father so as to be able to inform the court whether the father proposes to apply for any orders under the Children Act 1989.

The reporting officer will return the witnessed agreement forms to the court prior to the hearing. The justices' clerk should make it clear whether or not the reporting officer is required at the hearing.

ADOPTION AGENCIES

The Children Act 1975 provided for the formal establishment of 'adoption services' as part of every local authority's social services function. Existing adoption societies were made subject to control and approval by central government. The Adoption Act 1976 states that it is the duty of every local authority to establish and maintain in their area a service designed to meet the needs, in relation to adoption, of:

- children who have been or may be adopted
- parents and guardians of such children; and
- people who have adopted or may adopt a child.

The local authority has to provide these facilities itself, or ensure that they are provided by an approved adoption society. The necessary facilities include counselling, assessment of children and prospective adopters, and arrangements for placing children for adoption. Other organizations are governed by the Adoption Agency Regulations 1983. Both the adoption services of local authorities and approved adoption societies are called 'adoption agencies'. *Only* adoption agencies can make arrangements for adoption unless the proposed adopter:

- is a relative of the child; or
- acting in pursuance of an order of the High Court.

Adoption agencies have various statutory duties and responsibilities comparable to those for local authorities mentioned above. Both must establish an adoption panel of seven to ten members—and nominate at least one doctor to be the agency's medical advisor. There must also be a legal advisor, who need not be a member of the panel. The panel must consider the circumstances of *every case* referred to it by the agency and make a recommendation—whether or not adoption or freeing for adoption is in the best interests of the child,

127

and whether a prospective adopter is suitable as a parent for a particular child. The agency must make the final decision.

Protected children

An adoption order cannot be made in respect of a child not placed by an adoption agency unless the applicant has, at least three months before the date of the order, given written notice to the local authority within whose area he or she has his or her home, of the intention to apply for an adoption order. On receipt of this notice the authority must investigate and submit a report to the court. The other consequence of giving notice is that the child becomes a 'protected child'. This means that the authority have a duty to the child—including to visit him or her from time to time to ensure his or her well being. This protected status comes to an end if no application for an order is made within two years of when notice is given.

Children placed for adoption by an adoption agency are *not* protected children. However, if a child *is* placed by such an agency, then within six weeks of receiving the notice of hearing, the agency is responsible for reporting to the court.

'Schedule 2 reports'

The report required of the local authority or adoption agency when it is responsible must cover certain specific items set out in schedule 2 to the 1984 rules. A copy of this report is sent to the court which is then under a duty to send a copy to the reporting officer or guardian. Reports are confidential to the court. No-one else is given a copy. Directions regulating disclosure can, again, be given.

CONFIDENTIALITY

It is important that a child knows the truth about his or her origins and there are benefits, in appropriate cases, of retaining contact with the natural parents and family. Nevertheless, a veil of confidentiality surrounds the adoption process, for example:

- applicants who wish their identity to remain confidential can request that they be allocated a serial number. This will then be used in all documents likely to be seen by the natural family. Courts must be careful not to inadvertently reveal details of such adopters
- the Magistrates' Courts Act 1980 sets out who in general may be allowed into a family proceedings court (see *Chapter 3*). This is further restricted in the case of adoption, so that, in effect, only

the applicants, respondents and people directly concerned can be there. There can only be extremely limited reporting of any adoption matter

- there is provision for an adopted person to seek access to his or her birth records once he or she attains the age of 18 years. This is subject to the applicant receiving counselling, either on a voluntary basis or on a compulsory basis if adopted before 12 November 1975 (the date that the Children Act 1975 received Royal Assent). That Act introduced the idea, following the Houghton Report, of 'greater openness about adoption'. In the case, for example, of a disturbed person seeking to trace his or her natural parents, case law provides that the record may be withheld where there is a real risk of a serious crime being committed or a serious danger to members of the public

- when an adoption order is made, a copy of the order together with the child's birth certificate is sent to the Registrar General and there is an Adopted Children Register index which is open to inspection. Anyone can apply for a certified copy of an entry in that register. However, the link between the register and the original entry in the Register of Births is not open to public inspection. The only exceptions are the provision of information necessary to enable an adopted person to obtain a copy of the record of his or her birth or under court order. If there is some risk from the natural parent then the High Court can use its inherent jurisdiction to order that anyone applying for details from the Adopted Children Register must seek the leave of the court

- the Children Act 1989 introduced an Adoption Contact Register. Natural parents and relatives can register the fact that they wish to contact an individual who was adopted. The applicant's name is entered in the register and the adopted person must also give notice that he or she wishes to contact any relative. The Registrar General then transmits to the adopted person the name and address of any relative on the register, and the decision is left to the individual who was adopted whether or not to make contact. The case of *Re L (Adoption: Disclosure of Information)* (1997), *The Times*, 9 January 1997 makes it clear that although the 1976 and 1989 Acts established procedures whereby people who have been adopted can make contact with their natural parents, there is no corresponding right 'in reverse'. In *Re L* the natural mother applied for an order requiring the Registrar General to disclose entries. It was held that a natural parent wishing to make even indirect inquiries had to show:

—circumstances of an exceptional nature; and

—that contact would result in some benefit to the adopted person.

PARENTAL ORDERS

The Human Fertilisation and Embryology Act 1990 allows married couples to make arrangements for a child to be born by artificial means and then to apply to a court for a 'parental order'. This confirms that the child is the child of the applicants. The Parental Orders (Human Fertilisation and Embryology) Regulations 1994 and the FPC rules also provide procedural guidance. Certain conditions must apply:

- the couple must be married and make application together
- they must be 18 years of age or over
- they must be domiciled in the United Kingdom, Channel Islands or Isle of Man
- the application must be made within six months of the birth
- the child must be living with the applicants
- the child must be the result of the husband's sperm or the wife's egg, or both, although carried by another woman
- the 'father' or the woman who carried the child must freely and with full understanding agree unconditionally to the order being made. This does not apply if a man has donated sperm anonymously. As with adoption, the woman cannot give her agreement until six weeks after the birth
- no money or other benefit must be given or received. Reasonably incurred expenses *are* allowed and a court can authorise such payments or benefits.

Procedure
The husband and wife apply using a prescribed form. The natural mother and her husband are the respondents. The proceedings are 'specified proceedings' (see *Part Two* of this handbook) and therefore the court must, on receiving the application, consider the appointment of a guardian ad litem. In particular, the guardian must investigate whether there would be any reason to refuse the application in the interests of the child's welfare.

The Adoption Act 1976 criteria (above) apply and the court must have regard to all the circumstances and give first consideration to the need to safeguard and promote the welfare of the child throughout his or her childhood.

The agreement of the natural mother and father has to be obtained and can be in writing. As the guardian has a duty to investigate the issue of consent, it is possible for the guardian to use his or her experience as reporting officer in adoption proceedings and to adapt the consent form used for adoptions.

Effect of a parental order
The order gives parental responsibility to the husband and wife and extinguishes the parental responsibility of any other person. The child is thereafter treated as the applicants' child. The Registrar General is informed and makes an entry in a Parental Order Register—and marks the original entry in the Register of Births 're-registered'. As with adoption, there are provisions about access to copies of entries in the register and disclosure of birth records to people subject to parental orders.

Family proceedings
The definition of family proceedings in the Children Act 1989 was extended to include applications for parental orders. The court therefore has power to make orders of its own motion under section 8 of that Act: see *Chapter 2*.

If the statutory conditions are not met for some reason—and the court refuses the application—the applicants can, instead, apply for an adoption order. Although the same criteria apply to both adoption orders and parental orders, an adoption order may, for example, be granted on the consent of the mother being dispensed with, which is not possible in parental order proceedings.

INTERNATIONAL ADOPTIONS

Adoptions in respect of children brought into England and Wales from overseas can be complex and would not normally be dealt with in a family proceedings court: seek legal advice.

PART TWO: Materials

A Application Form: Children Act 1989 (and Supplement for Care or Supervision Order) *135*

B Specimen Directions *142*

C Best Practice Notes
  - *For the Judiciary and Family Proceedings Courts When Ordering a Welfare Report (and Pro Forma) 146*
  - *To Court Staff When Welfare Reports Have Been Ordered 150*

D Form to Accompany Direction to Investigate under Section 37 Children Act 1989 *151*

E Definitions: Family Proceedings; Specified Proceedings *153*

F Decision Making *156*

G Findings of Fact and Reasons *160*

H Guide to Lawyers on How to Prepare for Trial *163*

I Experts: Role and Court Expectations *164*

J Specimen Form of Undertaking *166*

Materials A *Application Form: Children Act 1989 (and Supplement for Care or Supervision Order)*

As explained in *Chapter 3*, all Children Act 1989 cases involve the use of prescribed forms (which are common across all courts dealing with family matters). Only these forms can be used. Magistrates should read the completed application along with other core documents before sitting in court to adjudicate. Form C1 is the core application form used in all types of Children Act application. Sometimes a supplement has to be completed by the applicant. An example is Form 13 below.

Application for an order	**Form C1**
Children Act 1989	

The Court	**To be completed by the court**
	Date issued
	Case number
The full name(s) of the child(ren)	Child(ren)'s number(s)

---

1 About you (the applicant)*

State
- *your title, full name, address, telephone number, date of birth and relationship to each child above*
- *your solicitor's name, address, reference, telephone, FAX and DX numbers.*

*A revised draft (May, 1997) will in due course require the disclosure of criminal convictions or pending prosecutions.

2 The child(ren) and the order(s) you are applying for

For each child state
- *the full name, date of birth and sex*
- *the type of orders you are applying for (for example, residence order, contact order, supervision order).*

135

3 Other cases which concern the child(ren)

If there have ever been, or there are pending, any court cases which concern
- *a child whose name you have put in paragraph 2*
- *a full, half or step brother or sister of a child whose name you have put in paragraph 2*
- *a person in this case who is or has been, involved in caring for a child whose name you have put in paragraph 2*

Attach a copy of the relevant order and give
- *the name of the court*
- *the name and panel address (if known) of the court welfare officer, if appointed*
- *the name and contact address (if known) of the solicitor appointed for the child(ren).*

4 The respondent(s)

Appendix 3 Family Proceedings Rules 1991; Schedule 2 Family Proceedings Courts (Children Act 1989) Rules 1991

For each respondent state
- *the title, full name and address*
- *the date of birth (if known) or the age*
- *the relationship to each child.*

5 Others to whom notice is to be given

Appendix 3 Family Proceedings Rules 1991; Schedule 2 Family Proceedings Courts (Children Act 1989) Rules 1991

For each person state
- *the title, full name and address*
- *the date of birth (if known)or age*
- *the relationship to each child.*

6 The care of the child(ren)

For each child in paragraph 2 state
- *the child's current address and how long the child has lived there*
- *whether it is the child's usual address and who cares for the child there*
- *the child's relationship to the other children (if any).*

7 Social Services

For each child in paragraph 2 state
- *whether the child is known to the Social Services.
  If so, give the name of the social worker and the address of the Social Services department*
- *whether the child is, or has been, on the Child Protection Register. If so, give the date of registration.*

8 The education and health of the child(ren)

For each child state
- *the name of the school, college or place of training which the child attends*
- *whether the child is in good health. Give details of any serious disabilities or ill health*
- *whether the child has any special needs.*

137

9 The parents of the child(ren)

For each child state
- *the full name of the child's mother and father*
- *whether the parents are, or have been, married to each other*
- *whether the parents live together. If so, where*
- *whether, to your knowledge, either of the parents have been involved in a court case concerning a child. If so, give the date and the name of the court.*

10 The family of the child(ren) (other children)

For any other child not already mentioned in the family (for example, a brother or a half sister) state
- *the full name and address*
- *the date of birth (if known) or age*
- *the relationship of the child to you.*

11 Other adults

State
- *the full name of any other adults (for example, lodgers) who live at the same address as any child named in paragraph 2*
- *whether they live there all the time*
- *whether, to your knowledge, the adult has been involved in a court case concerning a child. If so, give the date and the name of the court.*

138

12 Your reason(s) for applying and any plans for the child(ren)
State briefly your reasons for applying and what you want the court to order
- *Do not give a full statement if you are applying for an order under Section 8 of Children Act 1989. You may be asked to provide a full statement later.*
- *Do not complete this section if this form is accompanied by a prescribed supplement.*

13 At the court
State   • *whether you will need an interpreter at court (parties are responsible for providing their own). If so, specify the language*
- *whether disabled facilities will be needed at court.*

Signed   Date
(Applicant)

EDITORIAL NOTE: The Children (Allocation of Proceedings) Order 1991 lays down the procedure for the starting of cases:

Private law cases The applicant can choose which court he or she wishes to start proceedings in. This 'freedom' is often curtailed if the applicant is legally aided. The Legal Aid Board will often limit the certificate to proceedings in the family proceedings court unless the applicant can show that it is appropriate for the case to start in the county court. The respondent, initially, has no say in the matter. The justices' clerk can allocate a *private law* case to another court in the interests of the child. The court can review this, or transfer cases: *Chapter 3.*

Public law cases Most cases must commence in the family proceedings court. Some cannot be allocated to the county court, e.g. emergency protection and education supervision cases. Most cases, however, can be allocated elsewhere if appropriate and the justices' clerk must consider this aspect. The magistrates may also consider transferring the case as it progresses if circumstances change.

Supplement for an application for a Care or Supervision Order

Section 31 Children Act 1989

Form C13

The court

To be completed by the court

Date issued

Case number

The full name(s) of the child(ren)

---

1 The grounds for the application

The grounds are   that the child[ren] [is] [are] suffering or [is] [are] likely to suffer, significant harm and the harm, or likelihood of harm, is attributable to

the care given to the child(ren), or likely to be given to the child(ren) if the order were not made, not being what it would be reasonable to expect a parent to give to the child(ren)

the child(ren) being beyond parental control

2 The reason(s) for the application

If you are relying on a report or other documentary evidence, state the date(s) and author(s) and enclose a copy

3 Your plans for the child(ren)

Include

- *in the case of supervision orders only, any requirements which you will invite ithe court to impose pursuant to paragraph, 1 Schedule 3 Children Act 1989*
- *in all cases, whether you will invite the court to make an interim order.*

4 The direction(s) sought

Family Proceedings Rules 1991 Rule 4.14
Family Proceedings Courts (Children Act 1989) Rules 1991 Rule 14

Signed   Date
(Applicant)

141

Materials B *Specimen Directions*

The family proceedings court, a member of the family panel, the justices' clerk or an authorised court legal advisor can give directions for the conduct of a case: *Chapter 3.* The following are some examples of the kind of directions which may be given. Many courts use pro formas and practitioners should enquire locally about whether it is the practice to make copies available.

•   •   •   •   •

In the   Family Proceedings Court   Case number

Full name(s) of child(ren)   Date(s) of birth   Child(ren)'s number(s)

_____   _____   _____

_____   _____   _____

The court directs that the time limit for serving notice of application be abridged to

•   •   •   •   •

The court* directs/grants leave that   (*i.e. *only* the court in this

                                                   instance, *not* the justices'

_____   clerk or legal advisor)

_____

be joined as (a) party(ies) to the proceedings

•   •   •   •   •

The court directs that the oral evidence which the parties shall be entitled to call at the final hearing of this matter shall be limited to those witnesses whose statements have been filed at court and served on all parties by the following dates:

Applicants by   _____

1st respondent by   _____

2nd respondent by   _____

Thereafter no further statements may be lodged with the court without the leave of the court.

•   •   •   •   •

The court directs that the (guardian ad litem)(court welfare officer) file a report
by 4 pm on
The guardian ad litem must attend the (final hearing) (next directions hearing)
The court welfare officer must (be available to) attend the (final hearing) (next
directions hearing).

• • • • •

The court grants leave and directs that the child(ren)

_____

_____

be (examined) (interviewed) by   _____

and   _____

and that (all) (the below mentioned) documents be disclosed to

_____ and to

_____

for the purpose of preparing (a) (joint) report(s). Any report which results from
this disclosure or examination must be filed at the court office and disclosed to
all parties by 4 pm on

• • • • •

The court directs that the parties consult for the purpose of jointly instructing
(an) expert(s) (in) (on the following matters)

_____

_____

The parties must consult by 4 pm on
and (the court will consider the matter further at the adjourned
directions hearing on   )
(The written agreement and nomination must be filed at the court by 4 pm on
                    for the approval of the clerk to the justices/authorised legal
advisor)

• • • • •

143

The court directs that the expert witnesses meet to discuss the areas of dispute revealed by the report(s) of (the expert witnesses). This meeting shall be within days of the report(s) being filed at the court office and disclosure of them to

_____ and to

_____

within   days of that meeting, and no later than
The solicitors for   must file at the
court office a statement agreed by the parties. The statement must state the issues which are agreed and those which are not agreed.

•   •   •   •   •

The court directs that the   serve and lodge a statement according to (the Family Proceedings (Children Act 1989) Rules 1991, rule 17(1)) (in support of)(in answer to) the application. The statement must be lodged at the court office by 4 pm on

The statement must be limited to findings of the report(s) with which (he)(she)(they) do not agree/relevant matters not covered by the report(s)/the matter of

•   •   •   •   •

The court directs that this application be listed for further directions on at The Court House   at

•   •   •   •   •

The court directs that this application be listed for final hearing on at The Court House   at

Time estimate

•   •   •   •   •

The court directs that the (child)(ren) (parties) need not attend court for the (directions hearing on   ) (final hearing)

•   •   •   •   •

144

The court directs that the (applicant) (1st respondent) prepare a concise chronology comprising

a summary of the history of the case
a schedule of the statements lodged
a summary of agreed facts
a summary of the issues to be resolved between the parties

The chronology must be lodged with the court office and served on the parties by 4 pm on

. . . . .

The court directs that a bundle of papers for the court be prepared. The bundle must contain the chronology and the issues, all exhibits, reports and authorities; the statements lodged by all parties. The bundle must be paginated and indexed. All parties must agree the contents of the bundle. The (applicant)(respondent)(local authority) must lodge the bundle with the court office by 4 pm on

. . . . .

Leave be given for the applicant to withdraw the application in respect of the child(ren)

_____ and

_____

(NB *Only* the court can allow withdrawal)

. . . . .

Leave be given to disclose papers to

_____ and to

_____

. . . . .

145

Materials C *Best Practice Notes*

The following Best Practice Notes were issued by the former Children Act Advisory Committee:

For the Judiciary and Family Proceedings Courts When Ordering a Court Welfare Officer's Report

1. A welfare report may only be ordered pursuant to section 7 Children Act 1989, i.e. when a court 'considering any question with respect to a child [under the Act] "requires a report" on such matters relating to the welfare of that child as are required when dealt with in the report.' A report may not be ordered for any other purpose.

2. Before a welfare report is ordered, consideration should be given to the court's power to refer parties to mediation (with the consent of the parties). This may be to a mediation service or the court welfare officer, depending on local arrangements. It is important that this should not be confused with a welfare report and that any court welfare officer who may have been involved in any privileged mediation proceedings should not be the officer who undertakes the preparation of a welfare report.

3. The ordering of a welfare officer's report is a judicial act requiring inquiry into the circumstances of the child. A report should never be ordered when there is no live issue under the Children Act before the court; for example, a report must not be ordered when no formal proceedings have yet been instituted. Furthermore, save in exceptional circumstances, a report should not be ordered in response to a written request by the parties.

4. Although the exact procedures in different courts vary, there will always be some kind of preliminary appointment or hearing before the district judge, justices' clerk or family proceedings court in children's cases. This is normally the occasion on which a welfare report should be ordered. The attendance of the parties and their solicitors is required at this time to enable the court properly to inquire into the issues to be covered in the report. When a court welfare officer is present, or otherwise available, the court may consider inviting the parties to have a preliminary discussion with him or her.

5. When a welfare report is ordered the judge, district judge or justices' clerk should explain briefly to the parties what will be involved and should emphasise the need to cooperate with the welfare officer and specifically to keep any appointments made. In particular, when the principle of contact is in dispute the parties should be told that the welfare officer will probably wish to see the applicant parent alone with the child. It should also be emphasised that the

report, when received, is a confidential document and must not be shown to anyone who is not a named party to the application.

6. The order for the report should specify the time by which the report should be filed and if possible indicate the date of the substantive hearing. The solicitors for the applicant should be handed a pro forma in the form of the model attached and asked to complete details such as name, address and telephone number on the front of the form. The judge, district judge or justices' clerk should complete the rear of the pro forma which sets out the reasons for the report and the concern of the court; this should set out succinctly the issues as to which the officer is being asked to report. This part of the form should specify any documents which are to be sent to the welfare officer. This form must be fully completed and attached to the court file before the court disposes of the case.

7. An addendum report may be ordered, e.g. for the purpose of testing an agreement between the parties or where there has been a substantial change in circumstances. However, an addendum report should not be ordered merely because of a delay or adjournment in the listing of the substantive hearing.

8. The court will not order both a welfare officer's report and section 37 report.

9. It should be noted that court welfare officers do not travel outside the United Kingdom; International Social Services are available to meet this need.

10. A court welfare officer will not attend a hearing unless specifically directed to do so by the court (Family Proceedings Rules, rule 4.13). When such a direction is given the court should ensure that the officer gives evidence as soon as possible after the case has opened (and in any event on the first day) and is released after that evidence has been completed.

Welfare Report Referral

About this form
The solicitor for the applicant must
fill in part 1 [below].
A judge or clerk to the justices
will fill in Part 2 [overleaf].
The court office will then send a copy
of this form and any other papers to
the court welfare officer within whose
area the child lives. This will be done
within 48 hours.

Court ....
Case Number ....

Name of judge or ....
Clerk to the justices ....

Date of case review ....

Date of final hearing ....
Report ordered on ....
This form sent on ....
Report to be filed by ....

Part 1
The Applicant

Full name [surname in BLOCK LETTERS] ....

Date of birth & relationship to the child   Date of birth ....   Relationship ....

Address
Daytime telephone number   Home ....   Work ....

The Applicant's Solicitor
Name and Reference   ....   Ref: ....

Address   ....

Telephone & Fax numbers   Telephone.......................   FAX ....

The Respondent

Full name [surname in BLOCK LETTERS] ....

Date of birth & relationship to the child   Date of birth ....   Relationship ....

Daytime telephone number   Home ....   Work ....

The Respondent's Solicitor
Name and reference   ....   Ref: ....

Address   ....

Telephone & Fax numbers   Telephone ....   FAX ....

Other relevant parties

Name (surname in BLOCK LETTERS)   ....

Date of birth   ....

Address   ....

....

....

Children

Name	Date of birth	Residing with	School attended
1	....	....	....
2.	....	....	....
3.	....	....	....
4.	....	....	....

The nature of the application
For example: residence, contact,
parental responsibility, prohibited steps,
specific issues, [or other]

The welfare report
Give, in detail the reason[s] for the court ordering
the report/particular areas of concern which are
to be reported on.

About the parties
Were they interviewed at court?   No   Yes

The family court welfare officer (name)
Was a settlement or mediation
attempted?   No   Yes

The family court welfare officer (name)

Have the parties been given copies of the information leaflet?   No   Yes

Are there any dates when the parties
will not be available?   No   Yes

The dates ....

....

....

Will an interpreter be needed?   No   Yes
The language(s) (including signing)

Are there issues of culture or religion
which the Family Court Welfare Officer
should be aware of?   No   Yes

The issue(s)

Are other papers attached to this form?   No   Yes

The papers are the court order +

149

For example: statements, directions.

Is there a child protection issue?   No   Yes

The Court Welfare Officer is

Give the name and address

Part 2 completed by   Name: Date:

                                        [District] Judge   Justices' clerk

To Court Staff When Welfare Reports Have Been Ordered

1. Staff should ensure that the pro forma on the court file has been fully completed by the solicitors and the judge, district judge or justices' clerk on the day that a welfare report is ordered. When this has not been done the file should be immediately referred back to the judge or, when he or she is not immediately available, to another family judge or authorised clerk.

2. A copy of the order and of the pro forma should be sent by the court to the court welfare office within whose area the child lives, within 48 hours of the order being made. Copies of all documents specified on the pro forma should accompany the order. The pro forma should be date stamped with the date of despatch.

3. When a welfare report is received, it should immediately be date stamped and copies should be sent by the court to the solicitors for the parties immediately (or faxed when there is less than seven days before the hearing) usually without reference back to the judge. Where a party acts in person a letter should be sent by the court inviting that party to call to collect the report.

4. When a hearing date (or change of date) is being considered and it appears that the parties will require the court welfare officer to attend, he or she should be consulted before the date is fixed.

Materials D *Form to Accompany Direction to Investigate under Section 37 Children Act 1989*

Certain duties to investigate the circumstances of children are cast on local authorities by the Children Act 1989. The court can also direct such an investigation, when the authority must then consider whether it should apply for a care order or a supervision order, provide services or assistance to any child concerned, or take other appropriate action: *Chapter 2*. No form is prescribed by any statutory rules. The form below indicates what instructions and information need to be given to the local authority.

From: **Family Proceedings Court**

To:

Direction for Investigation under Section 37 Children Act 1989

CASE INFORMATION

Child(ren)'s No(s):_____

Date of direction: _____ Legal advisor: _____

Date of next hearing: _____

Report from local authority to be filed by: _____

Nature of current proceedings (e.g. contact, residence etc.) and why the court considers that an investigation should be made:

_____

_____

_____

_____

Applicant's name: _____ Date of birth: _____

Address: _____

Relationship to child(ren): _____

Solicitor: _____ Telephone/Fax/DX No(s): _____

Respondent's name: _____ Date of birth: _____

Address: _____

Relationship to child(ren): _____

Solicitor: _____ Telephone/Fax/DX No(s): _____

Other relevant parties/information: _____

CHILD(REN)

Name	Date of birth	Residing with	School

Details of Interim Order(s) (if any): _____

Guardian ad litem appointment: Yes/No (where ICO made or considered)

Name of Guardian _____

```
PARTICULAR AREAS OF CONCERN RELATING TO THE WELFARE OF THE
                        CHILD(REN)
```

Issues of culture or religion of which local authority should be aware:

_____

_____

Copies of the following documents are attached:

DIRECTION UNDER S.37
APPLICATION
RESPONDENT'S ANSWERS
STATEMENTS OF:

_____

_____

DIRECTIONS
COURT ORDER(S)

Signed: _____   Date: _____

Designation: _____

Materials E *Definitions*

Family Proceedings

The term 'family proceedings' really has three definitions

1 *Under the Children Act 1989: section 8*
'Family proceedings' is defined by section 8(3) of the 1989 Act as meaning any proceedings 'under the inherent jurisdiction of the High Court in relation to children' or proceedings in enactments listed in section 8(4). These enactments (various of which are mentioned in this handbook) are:

Parts I, II and IV of the 1989 Act
Matrimonial Causes Act 1973
Domestic Violence and Matrimonial Proceedings Act 1976*
Adoption Act 1976
Domestic Proceedings and Magistrates' Courts Act 1978
Sections 1 and 9 Matrimonial Homes Act 1983*
Part III Matrimonial Proceedings Act 1984

Also, when implemented, this list will include applications under the Family Law Act 1996 (see schedule 8, paragraph 60 Family Law Act 1996) but items marked with an asterix will be deleted.

In this context, when any court is dealing with 'family proceedings' it can, when a child is involved, make any section 8 order irrespective of whether any application has been made for such an order (see *Chapter 2*). In addition, in any family proceedings in which a question arises in respect of the welfare of the child by virtue of section 37 of the 1989 Act, if it feels it might be appropriate for a care or supervision order to be made in respect of the child, the court may direct the appropriate local authority to investigate the child's circumstances.

2 *Under the Children Act 1989: section 92*
This provision, which deals with the jurisdiction of courts, changed the terminology from 'domestic proceedings' to 'family proceedings'. Section 92(2) provides that 'Proceedings under this Act shall be treated as family proceedings in relation to magistrates' courts'.

It was held in *R (J) v Oxfordshire County Council* [1992] 3 All ER 660 that the Children (Admissibility of Hearsay Evidence) Order 1991 which allows hearsay in relation to 'family proceedings' applied to secure accommodation applications. The latter do not fall within section 8(4) as only Parts I, II and IV of the Children Act 1989 are mentioned and applications for secure accommodation orders are made under section 25 (which is in Part III of the 1989 Act). Nevertheless it was held that the wider definition of 'family proceedings' in section 92(2) should be used when interpreting the 'hearsay order' *Chapter 3*.

3 Under the Magistrates' Courts Act 1980: section 65

Section 65 defines 'family proceedings' under the 1980 Act (e.g. for the purposes of who is allowed to enter court, etc: see *Chapter 3*). The list is extensive and the provision also allows a court before which certain proceedings which can be dealt with by an ordinary magistrates' court—such as enforcement and variation applications in respect of orders for financial provision—to treat those proceedings as family proceedings for the purposes of the 1980 Act: for more detailed information about the extent of section 65 and its implications seek legal advice.

Specified Proceedings

Certain consequences follow if proceedings are 'specified proceedings':

- the child(ren) will be a party to the proceedings
- a guardian ad litem will normally be appointed
- the guardian will normally appoint a solicitor to act for the child

and see, generally, *Chapter 2*.

The combined effect of section 41(6) Children Act 1989, rule 2(2) and rule 21A(2) of the FPC rules means that the following are specified proceedings:

1. An application for a care order or supervision order under section 31 of the 1989 Act.

2. Where the court has given a direction under section 37 of the Act (i.e. a direction to the local authority to investigate the possibility of bringing care or supervision proceedings: see *Materials D*) and has made or is considering whether to make an interim care order in the meantime.

3. Proceedings for the discharge of a care order or the variation or discharge of a supervision order.

4. Proceedings by way of an application under section 39(4) of the 1989 Act where someone is not entitled to apply for a supervision order to be discharged, but is the person with whom the child is living for a supervision order to be varied as far as it imposes a requirement which affects that person.

5. Proceedings in which a court is considering whether to make a residence order with respect to a child who is the subject of a care order.

6. Proceedings with respect to contact between a child who is the subject of a care order and any other person.

7. Any proceedings under Part V of the 1989 Act. This includes applications for child assessment orders, emergency protection orders and applications to extend or discharge them, and applications for recovery orders:

8. On an appeal against:

- the making or refusal to make a care order, supervision order or any order under section 34 (contact with children in care).
- the making or refusal to make a residence order with respect to a child who is subject to a care order or
- the variation or discharge or refusal of any application to vary or discharge any order of the kind mentioned in sub-paragraph (a) or (b) above.
- the refusal of an application under section 39(4).
- the making or refusal to make an order under Part V.

9. Proceedings under section 25 of the 1989 Act (application by local authority to restrict the liberty of children in their care).

10. Proceedings under section 33(7) in relation to children who are subject to a care order when an application is being made to cause the child to be known by a new surname or remove him or her from the United Kingdom.

11. Applications under paragraph 19(1) of schedule 2 of the 1989 Act. This requires the local authority to apply to court if they wish to arrange for any child in their care to live outside England and Wales.

12. An application to extend or further extend a supervision order under paragraph 6(iii) of schedule 3 (a supervision order generally lasts for up to 12 months and applications have to be made if the supervisor or other person wishes to extend the order).

13. Applications under section 30 Human Fertilisation and Embryology Act 1990.

Materials F *Decision Making*

The following structure shows key stages of decision making in cases under the Children Act 1989 in the family proceedings court. It is based in part on a structure provided by Warwickshire Magistrates' Courts Service:

BEFORE COURT

1. Assembling for court
Assemble in good time (30 minutes before the court is due to start) and move to a quiet room with colleagues and the legal advisor.

2. Directions on previous hearings
Consider any previous directions made about e.g. the timetable, preparation of reports, filing of statements etc., and any previous interim orders.

3. Understand nature of application

- *Public law* or *private Law*
- Names and ages of children

--   ---------------------------------

--   ---------------------------------

--   ---------------------------------

- The applicant   Represented by

---------------------------   --

- *Ex parte/inter partes*

  If *inter partes*
- The respondent(s)   Represented by

-------------------------   --

-------------------------   --

-------------------------   --

- Other relevant people, e.g. guardian ad litem, welfare officer etc.

- People seeking leave to be made a party

- The application is for an interim order/final order

----

4. Preparation
If not already done, read and consider the documentation in the case, including written evidence and reports (case papers may be sent by post to magistrates on duty a day or so before the hearing).

5. The issues
In discussion with colleagues and with the help of the legal advisor seek to identify in brief:

- areas of agreement
- areas of disagreement
- critical issues not covered by statements or evidence
- the range of orders available.

6. Further information
Identify those areas where the court will seek further information in order to:

- decide on issues identified at 5(c) above
- clarify facts
- consider alternative solutions.

Questions must always be phrased so as to avoid any impression of pre-judgement.

IN COURT

7. Opening the proceedings
Chairman (or legal advisor as appropriate and according to local practice) to greet the parties, ask them to sit down, explain the stage the case has reached and what the hearing is intended to achieve that day. If necessary, ask people to introduce themselves or make introductions from the chair. Try to create a sympathetic atmosphere of calm and informality. If appropriate, the chairman should remind parties about the:

- welfare principle
- no order principle
- delay principle

- welfare checklist
- non-adversarial nature of the proceedings.

8. The hearing

The order of speeches and evidence will normally be as noted in *Chapter 3* unless the court determines otherwise. Evidence should be on oath (or affirmation) and as far as possible the chairman should seek to ensure that it focuses in on the areas of disagreement. No party to a case may give evidence on matters other than those contained in their written statement without the court's permission.

The President's *Practice Direction (Family proceedings: Case management)* (1995) 1 FLR 456 indicates that failure by practitioners in family proceedings to conduct cases economically 'would incur appropriate orders for costs including wasted costs'. The *Practice Direction* also indicates among other things that:

- the importance of reducing cost and delay means that courts should assert greater control over the preparation for and conduct of hearings than was hitherto customary
- courts would accordingly exercise their discretion to limit discovery, the length of opening and closing oral submissions, the time allowed for examination and cross-examination of witnesses, the issues on which they wished to be addressed, and reading aloud from documents and authorities
- unless otherwise ordered, every witness statement would stand as the evidence in chief of the witness concerned. The substance of the evidence which a party intended to adduce at the hearing had to be sufficiently detailed but without prolixity: it had to be confined to material matters of fact, not (except in the case of the evidence of professional witnesses) of opinion; and if hearsay evidence was to be adduced, the source of the information had to be declared or good reason given for not doing so
- it was a duty owed to the court both by the parties and their legal representatives to give full and frank disclosure. The parties and their advisors had also to use their best endeavours to confine the issues and the evidence called to what was reasonably considered essential for the proper presentation of their case, to reduce or eliminate evidence for expert evidence, and in advance of the hearing to agree which were the issues or the main issues
- unless the nature of the hearing made is unnecessary and in the absence of specific directions, bundles should be agreed and prepared for the court: see further *Materials H*
- the opening speech should be succinct. At its conclusion, other parties might be invited briefly to amplify their skeleton arguments. In a 'heavy case' the court might in conjunction with final speeches require written submissions including the finding of fact for which each party contended.

The President has indicated by letter to the Justices' Clerks' Society that the above principles apply to family proceedings courts as well as other courts in the system of family courts to which the original *Practice Direction* applied.

9. The chairman should ensure examination of the areas identified at 6 above at the appropriate point in the case.

IN THE RETIRING ROOM

10. Findings of fact and reasons

At the conclusion of the trial, magistrates must, in consultation with the legal advisor, record their findings of fact and the reasons for their decision. An outline structure showing the stages in this process is set out in *Materials F*.

11. Legal advice

Due to the intricate nature of many proceedings in the family proceedings court—and the way in which issues, evidence, fact and law are often interwoven—the legal advisor should be invited to be with the justices throughout their retirement. This is the only sure way to enable him or her to deal with those matters mentioned at item 10.

PRONOUNCEMENT

12. The chairman will make the pronouncement in open court in the form agreed by the magistrates and as recorded by the legal advisor (normally reading from what may be a detailed 'script'). The chairman should explain to the parties beforehand that this could take some time. If there are to be any further hearings, the timetable for this should be indicated and that it must be adhered to.

Materials G *Findings of Fact and Reasons*

Whenever making an order or refusing an application or request, the magsitrates hearing a case must, in consultation with their legal advisor, record their *findings of fact* (i.e. decisions about matters in dispute together with a note of items agreed by the parties) and the *reasons* in support of their decision: *Chapter 3*. To enable the legal advisor to discharge his or her duties properly, it is advisable for him or her to be present throughout the magistrates' deliberations: *Chapter 1*. The following structure is an example of a pro forma and is based on a *private law* application. Many courts use pro formas—often a range of these for various types of cases. Practitioners should enquire locally about whether it is the practice to make copies available.

FAMILY PROCEEDINGS COURT SITTING AT

JUSTICES FINDINGS OF FACT AND REASONS FOR THEIR DECISION IN FAMILY PROCEEDINGS

Date

Justices: 1.   2   3.

Legal advisor:

Child(ren) concerned: _____Age

_____Age

Application for:

By: Applicant

Represented by

Respondent   1)

Relationship to child

Represented by

Respondent   2)

Relationship to child

Represented by

We have had the benefit of seeing and hearing evidence from

1._____

2_____

3._____

We have also considered reports prepared by

1._____

2_____

3._____

WE FIND THAT THERE IS THE FOLLOWING (COMMON GROUND) (AGREEMENT) BETWEEN THE PARTIES (e.g. history of case, relationships, parentage of child(ren), length of marriage/cohabitation, date of separation etc. Any relevant facts not in dispute)

THE FOLLOWING MATTERS ARE IN DISPUTE

WE HAVE MADE THE FOLLOWING FINDINGS OF FACT (facts which the court has found proved on matters in dispute)

STATUTORY PROVISIONS, CASES AND OTHER SOURCES CONSIDERED:

a) Quoted by the applicant

b) Quoted by (the) respondent(s)

c) Referred to by the court

IN REACHING OUR DECISION THE WELFARE OF THE CHILD(REN) HAS BEEN OUR PARAMOUNT CONSIDERATION. IN PARTICULAR WE HAVE CONSIDERED THE 'WELFARE CHECKLIST' AS FOLLOWS:

Wishes and feelings
of child(ren) taking
account of ages and
understanding

Physical, emotional
and educational needs
of child(ren)

Likely effect on
child(ren) of any change

Relevant characteristics
of children, e.g. age,
sex, background

Risk of harm to
child(ren)

Capabilities of
parents and others

Range of orders
available

If welfare officer's
recommendation not
followed give reasons

WE HAVE DECIDED THAT (specify order(s) or no order)

WE CONSIDER THAT MAKING AN ORDER IN THE TERMS SPECIFIED IS BETTER FOR THE CHILD(REN) THAN MAKING NO ORDER AT ALL

OR

WE CONSIDER THAT NO ORDER THAT WE CAN MAKE WOULD BE BETTER FOR THE CHILD(REN)

OUR REASONS FOR THIS ARE

Materials H *Guide to Lawyers on How to Prepare for Trial*

In *B v B (Court Bundles Video Evidence)* 1994 1 FLR 323 guidance was given to lawyers on how to prepare a 'bundle' for trial (see, generally, *Chapter 3* and *Materials F*). This is summarised below in relation to documents as an indication of the standards magistrates will expect:

- when preparing a bundle careful thought is needed by solicitors, possibly in consultation with counsel or solicitors for other parties. Liaison and cooperation is needed and should occur in *good* time
- if the task of preparation is delegated to a junior then it is the responsibility of the solicitor or managing clerk to check matters
- documents must be *legible* and photocopies not truncated. If they are illegible or will not copy, then a typed version of the document should be provided
- documents should be put in a *logical* (usually chronological) order. The court should be able to read the documents 'from beginning to end'
- all bundles of documents should to be properly indexed: with a description of each document and the page on which it begins and ends
- bundles should be individually paginated: and everyone in court should have identical pagination
- solicitors having conduct of the litigation should prepare all bundles and distribute them after making a charge for photocopying
- thought should be given to the categorisation of documents and their distribution in the bundles, e.g. court orders/statements/expert and medical reports, etc.
- medical records must be legible and correspondence in chronological order. Documents in manuscript should be typed unless clearly legible.
- rigorous pruning of unnecessary material should take place and duplication should be avoided
- where possible the chronology prepared by the applicant should be cross-referenced to the relevant pages in the bundle
- a list of *dramatis personae* identifying parties and witnesses, and where their evidence is to be found, is extremely useful.
- there should *always* be a 'witness bundle'
- bundles should be able to lie flat when opened. Staples, paper clips etc. should be removed once the papers are in a file or ring binder
- documents which arrive or emerge during the trial should be paginated, copied, hole punched and inserted in a bundle at the relevant place and if possible the index amended accordingly
- documents which arrive or emerge during the trial should be paginated, copied, hole punched and inserted in the bundle at the relevant place and if possible, the index should be amended accordingly.

Further, special procedures, apply to videos: seek legal advice.

Materials I *Experts: Role and Court Expectations*

The President's *Practice Direction* on case management (see *Materials F*) instructs courts to reduce or eliminate the need for expert evidence. A number of cases (and the former Children Act Advisory Committee) have given guidance on the mechanics of obtaining expert evidence and about the duties of experts. The position is as follows:

Instructing experts and defining the issues for them

- medical and other experts must be fully instructed. The letter of instruction should set out the context in which the opinion is sought and define specific questions for the expert to address. The letter of instruction should identify relevant issues of fact to enable each expert to give an opinion on all competing issues. The court determining the facts can then consider *relevant* expert opinion
- the same letter should list the documents to be sent to the expert and careful thought should be given to the selection of relevant or necessary documents. To assist the expert, an agreed chronology and background history should be provided in the core 'bundle'. An expert should never be provided with an unsorted file
- the letter should always be disclosed to other parties — who should be invited to contribute to defining the issues — relevant documentation, background history, and questions to be addressed. This letter must be included in the bundle of documents for the court
- experts should not hesitate to seek further information and documentation when required. Such requests should form part of the court bundle
- doctors with clinical experience of a child prior to the proceedings should have all clinical material made available in advance of the hearing for inspection by the court and other experts (e.g. medical notes, hospital records, x-rays, photographs and correspondence)
- experts who give evidence must be kept up to date with developments in the case which are relevant to their opinions. It is the duty of the solicitor instructing the expert to provide such information. It is also the duty of the legal representative calling an expert witness to ensure that, in advance of giving evidence, he or she has seen all fresh relevant material and is aware of any new developments so that the expert can consider the effect on opinions previously expressed. It is unacceptable for an expert in a child case whose evidence is relevant to the outcome to give evidence without having read, in advance, the report of the guardian ad litem.

Duties of experts

- expert evidence presented to the court should be — and should be seen to be — the independent product of the expert, uninfluenced by the party appointing the expert. The expert should provide independent assistance to the court by objective unbiased opinion, in relation to matters within his or her field of expertise

- an expert should state the facts or assumptions on which his or her opinion is based and not omit to consider material facts which detract from the conclusion or opinion
- an expert should make it clear when a particular aspect is outside his or her expertise
- if an opinion is not properly researched by reason of insufficient data this must be stated with an indication that the opinion is *provisional*
- if at any time an expert changes his or her opinion on a material matter this must be communicated to the other parties and, if appropriate, to the court
- if an opinion is based wholly or in part on research conducted by other people this must be set out in the report, and the research relied on must be identified. The expert must be prepared to justify the opinions expressed
- in *M and R (Child Abuse: Evidence (1996)* 2 FLR 195 the point was made that in cases involving children expert medical and psychiatric evidence is often quite indispensable to the court. At one time it was thought that an expert witness could not give evidence of his or her opinion on an issue in the case, especially not when it was the ultimate issue, determinative of the case, for example, whether the child has been sexually abused. However, section 3 Civil Evidence Act 1972 brought to an end the rule that expert evidence on an issue in the case was not admissible. It *is* now clear therefore that such evidence is admissible as long as it is relevant. It was also emphasised in that case that although a court is entitled to receive such evidence, the weight it attaches to it is a matter for the court. The court must never lose sight of the fact that the final decision is for the court.

Materials J *Specimen Form of Undertaking*

Family proceedings courts will have jurisdiction to accept undertakings for the first time (and in limited circumstances) under the Family Law Act 1996: see *Chapter 7*. The following is the form of undertaking contained in the draft rules as at May, 1997.

In the   **Magistrates' Court**

                                                            Case Number

___

This form is to be used only for an undertaking, not for an injunction.

General Form of Undertaking
Family Law Act 1996

___

Applicant
Ref:
Respondent
Ref:

___

On the   day of

(1) Name of the person giving undertaking

(1)

(appeared in person) (was represented by (Solicitor) (Counsel)

(2) Set out the terms of the undertaking

and gave an undertaking to the Court promising
(2)

(3) Give the date and time or event when the undertaking will expire

And to be bound by these promises until (3)

The Court explained to (1)

the meaning of his undertaking and the consequences of failing to keep his promises

(4) The court may direct that the party who gives

And the Court accepted his undertaking (4)
(and *if so ordered* directed that

the undertaking shall
personally sign the
statement overleaf

(1)
statement overleaf)

should sign the

(5) Set out any other
directions given by
the court

And the Court ordered that (5)

Ordered by
On

Justice(s) of the Peace

Important Notice

(6) Address of the person
giving the undertaking

To (1)
Of (6)

- You may be sent to prison for contempt of court if you break the promises that you have given to the court.*
- If you do not understand anything in this document you should go to a solicitor, Legal Advice Centre or a Citizens' Advice Bureau.

General Form of Undertaking (Statement)

The court may direct
that the party who
gives the undertaking
shall personally sign the
statement opposite

Statement

I understand the undertaking that I have given,
and that if I break any of my promises to the court
I may be sent to prison for contempt of court*

Signed

Date

To be completed
by the Court

Delivered:

- By posting on:
- By hand on:
- Through a solicitor on:

Signed: (Officer)

Date:

* Editorial note: In the case of the family proceedings court, this should be taken to mean enforcement pursuant to section 63 Magistrates' Courts Act 1980: see *Chapter 6*

Index

A

abduction 89
abuse 102
acknowledgement of service 43
Adopted Children Register 129
adoption 10 12 29 119 131
    panel 127
Adoption Act 1976 119 130
Adoption Agency 119 120 127
Adoption Contact Register 129
adultery 72
adversarial approach 12 38
Advisory Board on Family Law 17
agreed orders 71 74
agreement 16 45 57 60 61
    financial provision 80
allocation 16 44
amendment 47
amount, financial provision 75
appeal 54 107
application 39 *et al* 135
arrears 91
arrest 116
assessment
    medical etc. 27 35
    orders 32
associated person 105 106
attachment of earnings order 78 89
    93
attendance, child 46

B

balance of harm 103 109
bar on applications 41
Basic Training Programme 13
Best Practice 11 57 64 146
blood tests 81 83 *et al*
breach of order 86
'bundles' 47

C

call-out 40
care centres 10 18 19
care orders 23 *et al* 140
case management 16 54 158

chairmen 13
child
    abuse 34
    assessment order CAO 32
    financial provision 71 81
    protection 32 63
Children Act 1975 119 126 127 129
Children Act 1989 9 10 11 20 37
    56 74 102 119 131 135 153
Children Act Advisory Committee
    17 46 47 52 53 64 68 69 86
Children and Young Persons Act
    1933 56
Children Panel 17 57
Child Support Act 1991 72 80 119
Child Support Agency CSA 11 71
    77 80 89 97
cohabitant 112
cohabitation 73
collecting office 16 78 90
Colwell, Maria 64
committal: see *imprisonment*
conciliation 12 61
conferring 54
confidentiality 37 63 64 69
    adoption 125 128
conflict 12 57 61
consent
    adoption 120 123
    agreed orders 71 74
    various requirements re child 29
consistency 18 38
constitution 12
constructive desertion 73
consult, duty to 30
contact 20 21 24 34 58 86
    126cooperation 12
Cornwall and Isles of Scilly 65
costs 54
    enforcement 92
counselling 102
county court 9 44 74 84 87
Court Welfare Service 11 57 59 60
criteria
    financial provision 76
    threshold, care 23 39 56
culpable neglect 95

custody
    default 86

D
declaration, parentage 81
declaratory orders 109
defined order 87
delay 26 47 56
departures (CSA) 80
depth of knowledge 14
deputy chairman 13
desertion 72
    constructive 73
directions 12 35 44 59 60 142
discharge
    care order by residence order 22
disclosure 47
discovery 47
disruption 42
distress 89 93
divorce 9 29 74 100
documents 48
domestic court/panel 10
Domestic Proceedings and Magistrates' Courts Act 1978 10 71
domestic violence 73 99 102 104

E
early assistance 60
education
    needs 59
    supervision orders 26
emergency protection order EPO 11 32 33 *et al* 40 102
enforcement 12 85 *et al*
evidence 12 46 *et al*
exclusion
    order 11
    requirement 102
ex parte application 40 41 45 107
experts 46 53 164

F
failure to provide 71 72
family/Family
    assistance order FAO 11 20 23

Court Business Committees 18 60
Court Forums 18
Court (Matrimonial Proceedings etc.) Rules 1991 71 79
court system 9
    Division of High Court 10
    hearing centres 10
    Law Act 1996 10 11 88 99
    Law Reform Act 1969 81 83
    panel 9 13
    proceedings 38 91 131 153
    proceedings court 9
Proceedings (Children Act 1989) Rules 1991 38
protection orders 11
support services 102
fees 39
financial provision 11 71 73 89
findings of fact 16 52 160
formula (CSA) 80
foster parents 22 42 72
Foundation Programme 13
freeing, adoption 119

G
GALROs 64 124
gender 68
Gillick principle 31
grounds (care) 23
guardian ad litem 16 18 32 39 42 45 54 57 64 122 124 130
    report 66

H
harassment 107
harm 23 24
hearing 48
hearsay 51
High Court 10 41 44 54 74 84 87 105 121 127 129
Human Fertilisation and Embryology Act 1990 130

I
imprisonment 89 95 96 98
informal meetings 101

injunction 87
interests of justice (section 6 orders) 75
interim orders/hearings 26 49 90
  financial provision 78
investigative
  duties of local authority 27 151
  role of court 12 20

J
Judicial Studies Board 14 15
jurisdiction 10
justices' clerk, role of 15 45 52
Justices' Clerks' Society 47 52

L
Law Society 17 57
leave 38 42 45 47 50
  to intervene 42
legal advice/representation 15 17 52 62 66 163
  aid 99 100
  defaulter 96
liability order 11 98
liaison 12
listing 52
living apart order 71 75
local authority 10 23 58
  inspection of records 66 67
  investigative duties 27
lump sum 73

M
Magistrates' Association 15 46
Magistrates' Courts Act 1980 10 85 154
  section 63 85
Magistrates' Courts (Adoption) Rules 1984 119 122
Magistrates' Courts (Blood Tests) Rules 1971 83
Maintenance Orders Act 1958 84
marriage and commitment 114
matrimonial home rights 108
mature children 31 33 41
means inquiry/report 91
mediation 12 61 99 100 102

medical 27 35 57 67 69 118
  adoption 121
molestation 12 103 104

N
National Standards 57 60 61 63 68
nominal order (financial provision) 78
non-molestation 12 103 104
no order 20 24 56
notice period 40
NSPCC 23 32 33 35 41

O
obstruction 89
occupation order 12 99 103 108
one third rule 77
openness 15

P
parentage, declaration of 81
parental orders 130
Parental Order Register 131
parental responsibility 20 24 28 et al 119
parents/parenthood 28 58
partnership 23 24 28 58
party/parties 41
  child, as 39
payment, orders for 78
pecuniary orders 71 85
penal notice 88
periodical payments 73
plans for child 24 39 42 56
police
  checks 63
  protection 32 36
  third party, as 105
private, seeing child in 48
private law 11
privilege, mediation 61
Probation Service 57 59
probation supervision 25
procedures 37 et al
prohibited steps 20 21
protected children 128

170

protected earnings rate 94
protection
  in home 99
  harassment 107
protocols 60
psychiatric/mental condition 34 57
  64 118

Q
quantum 75

R
race 58 68 125
reasons for decisions 14 16 64 160
reciprocal enforcement 12 92
reconciliation 12 79
recovery orders 32
Refresher Training 14
registered orders 84
Register of Births 129 131
Registrar General 129 131
regulatory order 109
religion 58 68 123 125
remission
  arrears 91 92
  fees 39
reporting officer 122 124 126
reserved decision 52
residence 20 21 25 30 88
respondent 41 42 43
  adoption/freeing 120 122
review
  care 58
  committal 97
revival 79
revocation 79

S
search
  for child 35
  of defaulter 92
section 2 orders 71
section 6 orders 71 74
section 7 orders 71 75
section 8 orders 20 21 40 50 63
section 63: see *Magistrates' Courts
Act 1980*

self incrimination 50
separate representation 68
serious harm 61
service 43 46
sexual abuse 67 70 102
short term orders 26
significant harm 23 24 33 35 36
  63 103 109 110
social worker 62
specific issues 20 21
specified proceedings 38 154
speeches 48
split hearing 46
standing orders 89
statutory rules 38
structured decisions 14 156
supervision orders 11 25 135
surviving parent/guardian 31
suspended committal 96

T
threshold criteria, care proceedings
  23 26 39 56
timetable 16 27 46
training 13
truancy 26

U
undertaking 115 166
unemployment 77
unique reference number 40
unmarried fathers 31 122 127
unreasonable behaviour 72
user groups 19

V
variation 79
violence 11 73 99 102 103

W
warrant
  distress 93
  emergency protection 35
  enforcement 90
wasted costs 47 54 158

welfare
  checklist 14 58 69
  officer 42 45 79
  principle 15 24 56 58 103 120
    123 130 146
  report 57 60 61 63 79 146 *et al*
Welfare Service, Court 11 57 59 60
wife, second 77
wilful refusal 95
wishes, children/parents 20 30 59
  65 67 68 123
withdrawing application 41
witness 43 46 47

Y
young defaulters 95

Waterside Press Handbooks

Introduction to the Family Proceedings Court is the third handbook in a series produced under the auspices of the Justices' Clerks' Society. The two earlier books in the series are:

The Sentence of the Court: A Handbook for Magistrates Michael Watkins, Winston Gordon and Anthony Jeffries. Consultant Dr David Thomas. Foreword by Lord Taylor, Lord Chief Justice. (Fourth reprint, 1996). ISBN 1 872 870 25 2. £10

Excellent *The Law*
An extremely clear, well written book *The Magistrate*
Every new magistrate should be given one *Justice of the Peace.*

Introduction to the Youth Court Winston Gordon, Michael Watkins and Philip Cuddy. (1996) ISBN 1 872 870 36 8. £12

A comprehensive, up-to-date and readable overview of its subject . . . Although there are a number of more substantial legal texts on youth court proceedings, this is the first that I feel places those proceedings sufficiently in context *Law Society Gazette*

A must for those interested in the work of the youth courts *The Magistrate*

An extremely useful and practical guide *The Law.*

A fourth handbook, *Introduction to Road Traffic Cases* Winston Gordon, Philip Cuddy and Andy Wesson is scheduled for 1998. ISBN 1 872 870 51. 1 £12

Some Other Waterside Press Titles

Introduction to the Criminal Justice Process Bryan Gibson and Paul Cavadino. Rarely, if ever, has this complex process been described with such comprehensiveness and clarity *Justice of the Peace* (First reprint, 1997) ISBN 1 872 870 09 0. £12

Introduction to the Magistrates' Court Bryan Gibson (Second edition, 1995) A basic outline — plus a *Glossary of Words, Phrases and Abbreviations* (750 entries). An ideal introduction *Law Society Gazette.* A book which many magistrates will wish to carry *The Magistrate.* Compulsory reading *The Manchester Justice.* (1995) ISBN 1 872 870 15 5. £10

Introduction to the Probation Service Anthony Osler. Includes the role of the Court Welfare Service in family matters. (1995) ISBN 1 872 870 19 8. £10

Domestic Violence and Occupation Orders Chris Bazell and Bryan Gibson. A key work for family law practitioners. The Family Law Act 1996, the associated regulations—and the important interface with the Protection from Harassment Act 1997. (Autumn 1997) ISBN 1 872 870 60 0. £18

Interpreters and the Legal Process Joan Colin and Ruth Morris. For all people who are interested in spoken language or sign language in the legal context. ISBN 1 872 870 28 7. £12

Criminal Classes: Offenders at School Angela Devlin. A wise and absorbing volume: if you are in any doubt about the links between poor education, crime and recidivism, read it: Marcel Berlins *The Guardian*. An extremely frank and interesting insight: Victoria Myerson *The Law*. A book of considerable public importance which calls for attention: Sir Stephen Tumim. (First reprint, 1997) ISBN 1 872 870 30 9. £16

I'm Still Standing Bob Turney. By a dyslexic ex-prisoner who now has a job as a probation officer. Of interest to all people concerned about crime, punishment and offending (1997). ISBN 1 872 870 43 0. £12

Until They Are Seven Judge John Wroath's absorbing account of the origins of women's rights vis-à-vis property and children. Written by the former senior family judge for Hampshire and the Isle of Wight, this work will be of interest to all people concerned with family matters. (1998) ISBN 1 872 870 57 0. £16

A to Z of Criminal Justice Paul Cavadino. A 'mini-encyclopaedia' of criminal justice terms and terminology. (August 1997) ISBN 1 872 870 10 4. £18

Prisons of Promise Tessa West. Foreword by Sir David Ramsbotham, Chief Inspector of Prisons. Seeks to identify and encourage the 'goodwill, energies and skills which might be maximised so as to make prisons *safe* and *purposeful* communities'. (August 1997) ISBN 1 872 870 50 3. £16

Tackling the Tag: The Electronic Monitoring of Offenders Dick Whitfield. A first treatment of a topic which will be of mounting interest as electronic monitoring of offenders is introduced across England and Wales from 1997. Thoughtful, informative, positive and constructive. (September 1997). ISBN 1 872 870 53 8. £16

Waterside Press, Domum Road, Winchester SO23 9NN Tel or fax 01962 855567. Cheques: 'Waterside Press'. Please add £1.50 per book p&p to a maximum of £6 (UK only: postage abroad is charged at cost)